MY ULTIMATE SELF

Elisa,
Wishing you abundant
joy and success.

Thank you for your
support and enjoy
becoming your
ultimate self.

Esther Lewartt

4. 10. 2023

MY ULTIMATE SELF

HOW DEATH BECAME MY MOTIVATOR

ESTHER E. LEWARS, ED.S.

I dedicate this book to the ones I love,
the ones I have loved and lost,
and the ones God has destined for me to love in my future.

To my dad in heaven, your hallelujahs are still ringing in my ears.
To Javanie, your essence will forever live on through my deeds.

To my mom, your help and prayers continue to make me who I am.

To my children, Alyssa and Ethan, you bring me great joy.
Thank you for teaching me to be a better version of myself daily.

To my accountability partner, I appreciate your desire for continuous improvement.

Contents

MY ULTIMATE SELF

My brethren, count it all joy when ye fall into divers temptations; Knowing this, that the trying of your faith worketh patience.

James 1:2-3 (KJV)

DISCLAIMER

I am simple but complicated. I am quiet, but I have a lot to say. Communication is vital, and I also want you to get me - mind, body, soul, and spirit. I am Jamaican, Caribbean, and American, but I first identify as a living Earth being. I believe in God and no longer fear death, at least not as much as I did before (smile). This is not an autobiography, and my recollection of the stories and events may differ from the actual dates and times, especially childhood references. Some names have been changed or not mentioned to project people's privacy. Ultimately, my intentions are pure, and I come in peace and with love.

According to my earnest expectation and my hope, that in nothing I shall be ashamed, but that with all boldness, as always, so now also Christ shall be magnified in my body, whether it be by life, or by death.

Philippians 1:20 (KJV)

INTRODUCTION

On Tuesday, July 19, 2022, I wrote this book's first words, "all my life, I have lived crippled by my fear of death." Sitting on the edge of my chair, I mentally prepared to sign off from my work computer, then the thought dawned on me, what if I die today? I paused, got flustered, then processed the moment. What if I die today while driving home? Passing away today would have been sad on many levels.

I started to reflect on my life. Entirely irrelevant, but I had left dirty dishes in the sink. My computer desk at home and digital space could have been better organized. I still had unpacked containers in my closets from two years ago when I moved out of my marital home. The subsequent regret was the entrepreneurial plans and projects I had thought about and explored but never implemented. It was even more challenging to visualize the pain that my family and friends would feel. Most disappointing was to admit that a year had passed since my grandnephew Javanie died, and I had not lived in his likeness as I promised myself. That is, to share joy, be thoughtful, and become a go-getter with a millionaire mindset. If I die today, those desires will forever be impossible.

Reflecting, I concluded that unexpected and untimely death has happened to many, including my grandnephew. As such, I dare not think that I was invincible. I say it is unexpected, but to whom? From a human perspective, losing a young child is heart-wrenching, but the event may be right on time according to their set chronological clock. Do we all have a set biological clock or limit on the number of breaths, hallelujahs, or curse word before expiration? I, Esther Lewars, love God and help people. I have a twenty-year educational technology career. I am an adjunct professor and a mother of a high and middle schooler. Yet, not even I, with all those attributes, am guaranteed a long, prosperous, and pain-free life. Would you agree? If you said yes, you are correct.

Death has no regard for anyone, and as Bishop TD Jakes often says, "bad things happen to good people." I have come to realize that the unpredictability of nature and human interaction is what makes life interesting. Since every moment could create a quantum impact, if we stopped living because we knew our death date, then in those last moments, we could have made the most impactful action that humanity so desired.

While still at my desk, I decided to have a heart-to-heart conversation with myself. I needed to confirm if I genuinely believed in God. If I did, I had to live my life demonstrating his power to protect me until it was my time to go. Life would happen. There would be moments of great rewards and an equal number of challenges.

The sure thing is that life experiences have proven that joy inevitably cometh in the morning. There is no more significant evidence than in Psalm 30:5 - "weeping may endure for a night, but joy cometh in the morning." The morning represents the season of hope that appears after weeping lasts for a night or two, even three. As long as you have your life, you can expect relief from your hurt or disappointments; joy will return. Even on my worst days, I must remain thankful and strive to live a joyful life as God intended.

This development phase requires me to stop fearing death and prepare for my ultimate transition. It is not an easy task to accept that the end will come. However, embracing this mindset is the first stage of attaining a mental strength that guides you through any difficult situation. When you compare disappointment or disagreement to death, there is no comparison. The temporary mishaps are not worth the negative energy and emotions that detract from your goal and purpose. These temporary acts should not dictate how you treat others daily.

While there would be much left undone if I died today, there is much worth celebrating. I have learned, loved, created, contributed, and accomplished much. I have helped many people and created opportunities with and for others. So, I continue to live grateful, joyful, calm, and at peace with the problematic situations God has brought into my life to strengthen my thoughts, heart, and ability to act in his likeness.

My demeanor and appearance are still a work in progress. Even now, I have moments of doubt, fear, and loneliness. Yet, I will forever aim to be the light that brings pure joy to others. My presence should not resemble the years of loss, hurt, and heartache I have endured and

5

overcome. I did not see my situation as a worthwhile lesson in my broken state and stages. So, I share this book to help you and others navigate your thoughts and emotions surrounding death or any emotional loss. As my deceased friend Marcella said, we must "normalize loss" and develop pathways to healing. Only then can we truly live and fully take advantage of experiencing heaven on earth.

Your interpretation of death may be different from mine. I see it as ending this life experience without knowing what is next. So, at my computer desk, I knew I had to act now. In this lifetime, I have one life, many unfinished goals, and an unknown amount of time to complete them. I recommitted myself to the task at hand.

I drove home, seeing the world in a different light. I began to write what is now my first published book. As you read, remember that the intent is to ultimately live with gratitude, an abundance mindset, and a heart of service so that it will forever be well with your soul. The question what if I die today should never evoke fear because you have favor with God (Luke 1:30). Most importantly, you took the necessary actions to become your ultimate self.

PART ONE

Acknowledging and accepting my past and present so I can move forward with clarity into my future.

Yea, though I walk through the valley of the shadow of death, I will fear no evil: for thou art with me; thy rod and thy staff they comfort me.

Psalm 23:4 (KJV)

CHAPTER 1

EMBRACING THE DARKNESS

Exploring and accepting the darkness that precedes the light is vital. The darkness is every disruption that unnerves your body, soul, and spirit. These disruptions appear as hurt, disbelief, loss, desperation, despair, or disappointment, leaving you questioning yourself, others, and God.

It is within the darkness that you understand the true meaning of life. You recognize your strength, build resiliency, and develop a strong belief and dependence on God. The darkness materializes in various forms and formats for everyone. For some, it relates to personal trials and illnesses, family issues and tragedies, or career struggles and disappointments. If you are lucky and God sees you fit, you will have a blended cocktail of the above. Simultaneously or in succession.

What is now my awakening process started as moments of darkness in 2018 when I turned forty years old. This year was also five years after my 90-year-old dad died in Jamaica. Forty and fabulous! I had grand plans and expectations for my personal and professional life. I was going to soar. With my years of education, work experience, and community service, why not? I had invested time, money, and social capital, so a return on investment was overdue. In addition, my two children, Alyssa and Ethan, were now ten and twelve, so I was beginning to feel a sense of relief and pride from their growing independence.

In hindsight, God had a completely different plan. He realized that my high expectations needed to be higher. Still, today, not knowing his blueprint, I sense that his intentions for my life require a certain level of mind, spirit, and soul development that I need to attain by traversing through the darkness. Neither will the darkness cease until I have surpassed the criterion required to be successful in my future journey. Schools should teach these crucial insights and awareness.

While you can learn from the experiences of others, I've found that first-hand knowledge is always the best. I wish it weren't, but walking through the valley is essential for the growth of humanity. It is natural to resist and cry for help when the darkness appears. Only later will you recognize the importance of the lesson and how it relates to the preparation of your next chapter. Until you pass the required tests, God cannot trust you with the responsibilities and rewards associated with the high goals and expectations.

If only I had this level of enlightenment when a series of unexpected events started within a few months of my fortieth birthday. I fell and broke my right big toe, which required surgery. My marriage was falling apart. After a year leading Computer Science Education at the NJ Department of Education as an intergovernmental loan employee, plans for district level career advancement did an inverted climb. Then naturally, depression began knocking at my door. My high expectations were now so low that I didn't see the purpose of life. All that I had worked hard to achieve meant nothing to me.

Back then, the pain medication from my surgery provided the best sleep and retreat from my reality. I felt like living forever in my dreams. I had lost the will to live, but you, as an observer, wouldn't have known it. I tirelessly served, nurtured, and helped everyone else. I could instinctively and creatively solve every external problem but could not fix my issues. I had failed myself. I felt unworthy and more like an imposter. If you can relate to this, you must also recognize that it is all a lie!

In the dark, your worst self will become your best friend. All your fears will often visit and offer you constant companionship. It will require a fight and complete surrender to move beyond your situation. I realized that I needed to audit my actual value and capability, confront my lackluster demeanor, and overcome my fear of death to start living and shining the light of God in me.

Amidst the darkness, we often search for solace and answers. As a child, I feared that the hovering trees would fall into my home during storms. My mother calmed those anxieties by teaching me the Lord's prayer and encouraging me to ask for forgiveness and a pure heart.

Even in the depths of darkness, glimmers of light will guide us toward our purpose. While I am still discovering my purpose, this book delves into my experiences with grief, death, and moments of profound realization. I found the motivation to pursue my ultimate self by visualizing my mortality. I hope my journey inspires you to accept your circumstances and act toward your ultimate self.

To every thing there is a season, and a time to every purpose under the heaven: A time to be born, and a time to die; … A time to kill, and a time to heal; … A time to weep, and a time to laugh; a time to mourn, and a time to dance; … a time to keep silence, and a time to speak.

Ecclesiastes 3:1-8 (KJV)

CHAPTER 2
IN GOD'S TIME

Have you ever questioned your being, felt anxious, worried, depressed, or constantly wondered about your future? Do you fear living in today's world due to the inundation of tragedies and violence? These include unfortunate accidents, domestic violence, suicides, homicides, school shootings, mass killings, police brutality, international wars, and disasters. Add terminal illnesses and the loss of loved ones to the list. Do you also desire to serve, achieve your goals, and live a free and fulfilled life?

Get ready to unlock your fears, restore your passions, and release the ultimate version of you that God envisioned when he formed you in your mother's womb. When in doubt, never forget Jeremiah 1:5, "before I formed thee in the belly I knew thee; and before thou camest forth out of the womb I sanctified thee, and I ordained thee a prophet unto the nations." You were born with a message or service that you must share with others in your community or worldwide.

If you have never encountered these feelings or experiences, be thankful but continue reading this book, as it will prepare you for the laborious moments yet to come. When they appear, do not resist but strategize and flow so that you can learn from the experience. For those who experienced these fearful thoughts, feelings, or emotions, recognizing when they began can be fruitful to your healing and progress. It is also essential to understand that tragedies and losses have happened since the creation of time. As such, be comforted that it is quite natural. I came across three bible verses that support these sentiments.

Genesis 4:8, "it came to pass, when they were in the field, that Cain rose up against Abel his brother, and slew him" was an example of a modern-day family feud. Imagine being the parent of Cain and Abel. How painful must it have been for one of your children to kill the other?

Another situation was the disaster in Genesis 7:24, where God instructed Noah to build the ark due to the unseen and impending flood, which "prevailed upon the earth a hundred and fifty days." This verse infers that when things happen, expect them to sometimes last for a while. The storms will happen, but they will end, and the sun will shine again. It may take 150 days, but it will eventually end.

Lastly, in Daniel 3:17, Shadrach, Meshach, and Abednego professed, "our God whom we serve is able to deliver us from the burning fiery furnace, and he will deliver us out of thine hand." Not only can God deliver you, but you shall also prevail without the hair on your head scorched. Some situations were meant to destroy us, but we overcame them magically, proving God's grace and intercession.

I may be repetitive but remember that challenges will come and may last for a while, but over time, God will preserve and deliver you from the enemy's dart. During an internal encounter, an issue must flow through you. Likewise, you must position yourself in an external battle to flow through the circumstance. Instead of fighting, just flow. Let the problem take its natural course. God is able. He may not fix your issues on time but he will do it in time. If you look over your life, you will acknowledge this is true. Count the situations where it should have been different, but God delivered you.

According to the Bible, there is a time to be born and die. There is also a time to keep silent and speak. I am intrigued by all four areas, especially death and the need to verbalize my thoughts. I have reached significant milestones and made outstanding achievements, yet I endured loss and death from my childhood. I have also been silent throughout my life. I recognize the importance of speaking up, shining God's light, and exploring death's impact on my life.

Then spake Jesus again unto them, saying, I am the light of the world: he that followeth me shall not walk in darkness, but shall have the light of life.

John 8:12 (KJV)

CHAPTER 3

RECOGNIZING THE LIGHT

Growing up, I always feared death while simultaneously perceiving glimpses of myself as a public speaker. The duality of this has always been a part of my core. I equate my mindset and thought patterns to a Pisces, whose sign is two fish swimming together in opposite directions. How have I survived the dichotomy of being two in one?

I aim to be authentic but often compromise my stance and veer in the opposite direction. I am the same but different, a sure sign of madness. Left unchecked, behaviors such as indecisiveness, feeling stuck, neutralized, and not wanting to rock the boat became my norm. These feelings have led me to seek a higher and deeper relationship with myself and God over the last three years.

Only recently have I realized that the Bible is the playbook of life. It informs readers about life's expectations through storytelling and narration. The first non-commandment lesson that resonates with me is that there is a time for everything. Another critical point is that life entails duality or opposites, as evident in our environment, physical forces, mental state, and existence.

The universe's natural opposition and laws mimic life's dual nature. There are two opposite ends to each spectrum. For example, in Genesis chapter one, in the beginning, God created heaven and earth and called the light day, and the darkness he called night. There are endless examples similar to night and day, like sadness and happiness, love and hate, and closed versus open.

I acknowledge that the dark is just as important as the light. In chapter one, I mentioned that you evolve to the next and ultimate version of yourself through the dark. The light and darkness coexist to create a balance required to become the person God intends us to become.

They say time waits for no one and that it continues through eternity. However, I realized that time ends and dies every second it passes. Each day starts like a child's birth and ends like an elder's death. Likewise, I must live a purposeful life and simultaneously prepare for death. Before I die, I must release all the talent God has given me. Like Queen Esther, I must rise and be a vessel for this time. Otherwise, I could be considered an unprofitable servant and "be cast into outer darkness," where I will forever experience weeping and gnashing of teeth for not using my talent (Matthew 25:30).

I will now speak to the light that guides my life. After a series of darkness, I now resonate with the light, joy, and peace God promised me. He has been my source and my strength. A bright light is shining inside and through me.

I have accepted that God has ignited me with a vision to speak publicly in front of thousands. As a child, the image of myself holding a microphone was unusual because I was known as a shy little girl. I also didn't sing or have any known talent. In addition, celebrity news and their paparazzi lifestyle convinced me that I didn't want to be famous. I feared the public becoming aware of my failures and faults. So, as a child, I imagined every reason to dismiss that insight of me speaking with a microphone.

In retrospect, I realized that I shied away from public speaking all my life. I would have the urge to say something but quelled it as I refused to raise my hand or speak up in class or a large group setting. I avoided church activities that required me to talk in front of the congregation. Still, the images of me standing in front of a crowd would frequently and randomly appear.

Today, it is all so clear to me. God wrote and divinely ordained my path. He ignited a spark and purposefully positioned and prepared me for that glimpse of my future that I completely ignored. Being enlightened, I can attest that your path is also ordained; for some, the revelation is forthcoming. My faith is more sustained than ever before.

My introduction to stage performance and public speaking started when I wrote and performed my talent piece for the Ms. Jamaica Independence Pageant New Jersey in 1998. The poem was called *"The Youths of the Nation."* The writing was easy, but performing it with authenticity was nerve-racking. Even then, I seemed to have realized that I needed to challenge and channel my innate destiny of sharing my thoughts and voice.

A year later, I enrolled in a speech class at Rutgers University, where I sang "My Heart Will Go On" from the Titanic movie for my final assessment. I had never sung before to a crowd, but destiny unknowingly aligned and ordered my steps just to do it. It was a cathartic experience. I encourage you to challenge your inner critic routinely.

Lastly, agreeing to teach a university course that meets once a week for three hours was nothing but God planning my steps. I practiced my public speaking, developed my voice, and gained the confidence to talk to an audience. Eight years as an adjunct professor has been a mutual exchange of service and personal development.

My mode of operation is to stay in my lane and proceed cautiously, rarely going outside the box. It's like going ice skating but hugging the side of the ring all the way around. So much of this resonates with my Pisces sense of balance and the need to feel secure. My feet must feel anchored. Willing to take calculated risks and indulge in just the right amount of danger to keep on the straight path. For me, needing to see the breadcrumbs back to the village is the security that builds the bridge to continue exploring new lights and desires.

My journals and lengthy social media posts always reminisced my writing ability. In high school, my 11th-grade language arts teacher read one of my assignments and stated that she felt she was reading the story of a published author. I was surprised and pleased, but I must not have been passionate enough to act on her praise and develop my writing craft. The flicker of being on stage and exploring my writing talent soon disappeared as life became a reality. One thing is for sure; I never doubted that there was something special in me and about me. Unfortunately, I questioned my being, especially when others I respected did not recognize my light as I expected.

I am delighted that today is the day I release all doubt and begin solidifying my journey, wherever it takes me. Just as words form unintended silhouettes on a page, so are the mysteries of life that create equifinality, an information systems term meaning multiple paths to an outcome. Life presents limitless, unknown ways toward the person God intends me to be. Only at my death will I know the ultimate effect of my emitted light.

I started the writing process, but I resented my hesitation. My limiting beliefs told me I was not fully committed to the journey. My writing would be another unfinished project, or a long electronic note destined for the archive. Was I capable of writing and publishing a book on time? If you are reading this, I was persistent and completed the task, which started at the end of a workday on July 19, 2022. Since then, I have found every opportunity to write fervently. Instead of my lunchtime walks, I write. I write at my son's lacrosse games, during my daughter's tennis practice, and while waiting in the car to pick up the kids from their dad's house. Early morning and late at night, I write, revise, and design.

Coincidentally, my accountability partner Pavlok fueled this with a 30-day challenge to become a published author by August 31, 2022. He has an Amazon printed book, while months later, I continue to perform endless edits. I keep writing to share my lessons learned to help others transition from their mental or physical darkness to their light and purpose. If I do not share my story, I must at least share the goodness of God and his mercy thus far.

Behold now, I am old, I know not the day of my death.

Genesis 27:2 (KJV)

CHAPTER 4

WHAT IF I DIE TODAY?

What if I die today? Wait for it, wait for it, then exhale. Exhale because if you are like me, you have been holding your breath like a dead person for quite some time. I hate to think about death's finality, but it has been on my mind since childhood. Ironically, at the same time, I have avoided the topic of death instead of dealing with it. I have lived timidly, scared, and endured a subdued and cautious life. So, why did I decide to write about it now?

I have recently recognized the dual nature of death; the sadness it brings while reminding us that we must be more present and productive. This motivating element struck a nerve as I sat at my desk. Not just what if I die, but what if I die today or tomorrow? Some people leave home and never reach their destination, much less back home. If that happens to me, all the plans I have been delaying will forever be gone. I, therefore, felt a sense of urgency to act now. I decided that I must implement it now. I must create now. I must speak now. I must share now. Ultimately, death is the motivation to achieve God's destined purpose before it arrives. Because I know not the day of my death, I must live to live and live to die.

While I have had a constant, nagging feeling about death since childhood, it was always a figment of my imagination. It was an overwhelming thought and feeling that I had made up, one of my never-ending stories that I played over and over to myself. It was never evidence of things seen until it visited me frequently. Its visit began randomly, then expectedly, then often and unexpectedly. The unexpected encounters with death made the question "what if I die today" an important question. It was no longer a thought, but it was my reality. I realized that I, too, could depart at any moment. Therefore, preparing to become the ultimate version of my earthly being was essential. The counterargument could be that the quicker I reach my intended purpose, the faster I will get to my departure date. Who knows? I certainly do not.

During the last five years, I experienced a period of deconstruction, or as I would call it, my unbecoming. While Michelle Obama was having her "becoming" book tour, I was steadily unbecoming. My life was unraveling mentally, professionally, personally, and financially. I felt stuck in a rut like a hamster on a wheel. In design and technology terms, this was the initial phase of God's revitalization plan for my life.

Recalibrating my foundation was necessary to meet today's standards and efficiency codes. I had gone off track from my intended design, and my unrest would not cease until my current program and functions matched the designer's plan. Making the improvements would allow me to transition to the next version of myself in this lifetime.

If my life followed the software development life cycle, my syntax needed to be updated. I required rigorous testing before deployment. While in the post-production stage, I may still require repairs and updates. I will even become outdated and decommissioned at some point. Through it all, I would have filled a purpose and generated joy while being used.

Managing technology for a school, I would store away devices that no longer worked. For environmental reasons, there is a formal process to discard equipment once they reach the last stage of the technology life cycle, the destruction phase. It's the stage that consumers rarely consider when devices malfunction or become obsolete. Yes, consumers can return an item to the manufacturer or recycle it, but have you ever thought about what happens to the device from then on? Knowing what happens, I see the similarity with the stage of dying. It is the area I am now intrigued by or simply accepting.

Some technology parts are necessary for the product to work, but ultimately, it is simply trash or scrap. On the other hand, some products contain high-quality materials that can be recycled, sold, and reused in future products. Likewise, at the end of someone's life, we recognize their flaws but acknowledge and focus on their high-quality characteristics.

Your qualities, deeds, and personality will be remembered and assessed as a human being. Your friends and family will have an easier time if you positively impact others and are not just a liability to society. As such, why not live to serve and be the missing resource to someone else's journey? Be the person who, when you die, others will want to reuse and replicate your values and standards.

Along my journey, I encountered elders who had reached a high level of spiritual maturity. They shared their enlightenment with me, but I did not fully understand the cause. Marcella was a school social worker who passed away from cancer. Her goal was to normalize loss, which I now believe is essential. I worked closely with her to host a conference at Essex County College in Newark, NJ. She collaborated with grief counselors and other professionals to work with high school students. Despite her passing, I still failed to comprehend the intent and significance behind her work.

My most recent experiences have allowed me to realize the importance of normalizing loss. Experiencing the loss of my father and grandnephew made Marcella's purpose relevant and valuable. I can attest that in life, experiential learning is critical. You do not understand or learn until you practice or become immersed in the situation.

The fascinating yet sad thing is that people have been enduring loss and hardship for centuries. So, I ask myself, how can I help others deal with loss when it's not my thing? I am not a licensed counselor, grief specialist, or pastor. I have never studied psychology or neuroscience.

My expertise is being a Jamaican immigrant and now a naturalized citizen. It's educational technology, K-12 computer science education, information systems, Google Suites, and PowerSchool. It's surviving a 16-year marriage and going through a divorce. It's serving on the Caribbean Commission, rebuilding my credit, losing weight, buying my dream car, and being a mother of two teenage children.

Does my scholarly knowledge extend to dealing with loss and preparing for the end of life? Perhaps this is the path that God is calling me to shepherd. I had experiences with death, but I never realized the impact of those experiences on my life and psyche until now.

As I explore my past, I aim to pour love, empathy, and compassion into my younger self. That little girl needs those resources as much as I do today. Strengthening my core makes the question, "what if I die today" irrelevant. I encourage you to do the same, find your fearful, broken moments, and embrace that version of yourself with all the missing resources. Doing so will create space for creativity, innovation, and the desire to focus on continuous, personal improvement.

Set me as a seal upon thine heart, as a seal upon thine arm: for love is strong as death; jealousy is cruel as the grave: the coals thereof are coals of fire, which hath a most vehement flame.

John 10:10 (KJV)

CHAPTER 5
INTERNALIZING THE IMPACT OF DEATH

For as long as I can remember, the idea of death has always unnerved me. As such, I've avoided discussing the topic, fearing it becoming a reality. A reality where there is no return or do-over. A reality where I will no longer exist and have no power over what happens next.

As I think about it, control or lack thereof may be a significant issue and why I am at this place. I have always positioned myself to be in control, steer the ship, lead the army, and get it done. Not maintaining control and orchestrating the lives and things around me leaves me barren and useless. The idea of death is the culminating effect of not being needed, and so that must be why I have hated the thought of death.

I also now realize that living my life doing, giving, and serving has been a selfish act of appeasing my desire to feel necessary. I have always needed to show up for everyone because I thought they expected me to. It was an unselfish act of unconsciously seeking appreciation and validation.

I will not divert from the original intent of this book to address the personal work required to transition to a mental state of being confident with your authentic self. However, my sister Maxine, a licensed counselor, pointed out that my birth order and being the fourth of five girls may have influenced my thoughts, perceptions, and how I view myself.

Today, I continue to think about what happens if I die. If I die, those internal and external expectations die with me. They may linger in the minds of others for a brief time, but that is it. So, in thinking about my future self, what if I live my life as if I am not constantly available to others? Instead, I live focused on prioritizing my needs and goals. I cannot serve and assist others if I am not the best version of myself. I must balance and gauge my devotion to being a partner, mother, employee, or commissioner. I can be a ride-or-die friend or family member when appropriate. When applicable, I can go above and beyond as an employee, an entrepreneur, or a mentor. These and more are key growth areas I will explore on my journey.

Two weeks before July 19, 2022, I had the impulse to start writing a book after the smell of cigarettes came up from the basement into my apartment bedroom. I have been around smokers but that evening the smell knocked the wind out of my nose and made me reflect on my life. Forty-four years old and starting over has been a challenging but necessary process. A part of me died when I moved out of my home. I walked away from my marriage and left so many things and memories behind. I even left my children behind since it was the height of the COVID-19 pandemic.

Calling a family meeting and telling the children that their dad and I were separating was an excruciating task. The entire process was enough trauma for them, so I preferred that they continued to live in their home, despite the distance between us. Whenever I questioned my intentions, I remember Brené Brown on an Oprah OWN episode who said, "something has to die for something to live." That is so hard to accept, but it is so true. Tears are swelling up in my eyes at this very moment.

I was willing to temporarily sacrifice a part of my life so that my whole self could live and be around for my children. The part of me that died when I moved out of my marital home gave birth to the me that I am now and will become. I saw a better version of myself on my dark, depressed days. She motivated me to be bold and courageous and leave it all behind. She reminded me that I had done well in all areas of my life but could achieve so much more. I had built a family and home before, and I now had the awareness to recreate the process better and more efficiently, if I chose to.

On my darkest depressed days in 2019, my two children should have kept providing the fulfillment I needed, but that wasn't the case. Life had begun to feel like the death from which I was running. Disappointments were too much, and my existence just became too heavy. I didn't see the purpose of being on this perpetual hamster wheel. My children eventually played an important role in seeking a better version of myself; someone who was happy, at peace, bold, and fearless. I needed them to see that model and understand the need to set expectations and establish boundaries.

My deceased father also appeared in my dream and said, " Esther, you have to go." That was the only time that he presented himself to me. If I didn't listen to myself, I had to listen to my dad. I knew I would eventually join him on the other side if I didn't heed his warning.

Sadly, despite overcoming the heaviness, I still resided in a place of constant inaction. I would commit to achieving a personal goal but stall after taking off. Why? Was it mental issues, unclear goals, or spiritual warfare? I knew how to show up for everyone, so why not for myself? Only recently did I explore how my fear of death was limiting my ability to produce for myself and live a fulfilled life.

First Appearances of Death

As a preacher's child, I know that the idea of death, doom, and damnation started in my mother's womb. I am sure I unconsciously heard the stories of revelation, the expected end of the world, and the surety that you were destined for hell with everlasting brimstone and fire if you didn't accept Christ as your Lord and savior.

My first knowledge of death was when my maternal grandfather Silvera Williams, affectionately called Uncle Silly, died of poison when I was only three years old in Jamaica. I am grateful to my eldest sister, Maxine Chin, who gave me a complete account of his death and its impact on the community.

Uncle Silly was home for an entire week with his daughter, Aunt Enid, who lived in Boundbrook, Port Antonio. On Friday, he went to the Musgrave Market in Port Antonio to see two friends visiting from Johns Hall, which lies in the hills of Portland, across from the Rio Grande in the Windsor area. They were happy to see each other and walked to their favorite bar on Williams Street, close to the market. They had no idea that they were meeting there for the last time. This scenario reminds me of the Lord's Supper, Christ's last meeting with his disciples.

One of my grandfather's friends who went to the bar had a dispute with another man from their district. The other man stole a cow that belonged to my grandfather's friend. The friend reported the matter to the police, and the court date was upcoming. The man planned to poison my grandfather's friend to settle the case. The man enlisted a mutual friend to visit the bar while Uncle Silly and his friends were there. I imagine they ordered a dark drink such as a Guinness or Dragon Stout. The mutual friend had a similar liquor bottle containing gramoxone, an herbicide/chemical used to kill grass. So, while they were in the bar, the mutual friend switched the friend's drink to the bottle with the poison.

Uncle Silly's friend started drinking the liquor, not knowing the mutual friend had changed the bottles. He soon realized that the drink tasted unusual. He then asked the lady friend who was with them to taste it. She agreed that it didn't taste right. Then it was my grandfather's turn. As he put the bottle to his mouth and tasted it, he conclusively agreed that the liquor did not taste as expected.

Can you guess where this is going? I can only imagine their conversation; some of it may have included a few Jamaican curse words.

33

They probably blamed the poor bartender for giving them 'spoiled' liquor. I wonder if the mutual friend was offered a taste, and when he left the bar. That evening, all three friends felt ill and went to Port Antonio Hospital, where they all died between Friday night and Saturday morning. I imagined their agony and the confusion surrounding the source of their pain. On Saturday morning, my aunt Brenda, my mother's youngest sister, came to the house to tell us that our beloved grandfather was accidentally poisoned.

The court case transitioned from theft to murder. The man who stole the cow and his accomplice took three lives suddenly and senselessly. Both men were executed, so a total of five lives prematurely ended. It was a sorrowful time for all of us.

As young as I was, I felt it, and we all missed our Uncle Silly. I did not understand why someone would be so cruel. Why would a person appear as a friend but have evil intentions toward you? Why jeopardize innocent lives in your pursuit of a target; why kill at all? Murder is nothing new under the sun; the bible shows many fights, battles, and direct murders. Today, this experience has shaped my ability to trust people. I question everyone's motive. I observe and observe. I suspect anyone who intentionally prepares me food or drinks.

Unfortunately, I have yet to develop the moral capacity always to refuse. So, I indulge and at least try to pray before consuming it. I should take a stance and be consistent. I should either not accept food or beverage from anyone or release the story of my grandfather's experience, live life, and indulge freely. I hope for the best but expect the worst. With my fingers crossed, I pray that history doesn't repeat itself twice in my lifetime. Here lies the root of my doubt, self-doubt, and inability to trust others. Without genuine trust, I cannot create authentic relationships and partnerships.

My sister Jackielow had a close friend named Paulette with a daughter named Natalie. She and I played, laughed, and had fun whenever she and her mom visited my sister. We shared a connection. Nothing could have prepared a four-year-old me for the news that her friend Natalie had died. If my memory serves me right, she died of asthma or an unexpected illness. These memories have been locked away for some time but have unconsciously shaped the person I am today. As I think about it, tears come to my eyes because none of the adults recognized the hurt that I experienced. No one helped me to process my emotions and feelings. I think it was during this period that I started to recede to my internal self. Looking back, I now understand the pain her mother and family endured after she died.

After my grandfather's death, Natalie's death was the second realization that human beings had limitations. I was not lonely; I had other friends in my neighborhood and my one-year-old baby sister. However, Natalie's death created a noticeable void. In retrospect, I wonder if my inability to connect deeply with anyone lies in my fear of reliving the hurt I experienced losing a friend as a little girl.

To others, I may appear strong, unbothered, and even unapproachable. On the inside, I am that person, that little girl, seeking to understand why I do not show up boldly and with confidence. Is this childhood experience one of the possible reasons for my lack of self-commitment and drive for life?

There was also a well-respected couple in Port Antonio. I didn't know them personally, rightly so because I was just a child. The husband had a fleet of transportation vans, so I would often see him. The wife seemed very private because I never recall seeing her outside. I admired the splendor of their home. It was far beyond the rented three-room house that my mom and four sisters shared. Pitched on the side of a hill, it curved around a corner. It was difficult to miss the lavish greenery on my left, even as I ran past the property at full speed on my way to school. I was often running late, of course.

I was shocked and traumatized when I heard they had found the wife dead with her throat slit. Who could have committed such a horrendous act? Especially in Port Antonio, where the crime rate was about 0.01%. That is not a fact, but crime did not exist in Port Antonio. Neighbors speculated that it was her husband who killed her.

If that were true, how could you kill the one you loved? Where there was once a loving relationship now exists an uncontrollable hatred. If you truly love someone, it should never get to a point where their mistakes or decisions deserve death. This tragedy created another impressionable memory and perspective of death. Is it possible that this could this happen to me?

Internalizing Death

Another childhood friend and distant cousin also died at the hands of her partner. Her family owned the house that my mom rented for years.

She left Jamaica for America when I was in elementary school. I never saw her again but instead heard the devastating story of her death. Her son's dad murdered her and left his child unattended with her body. The news of her death numbed me for a long time.

From that age onwards, I wondered if this could also happen to me. By then, my mind had so many negative thoughts about the world. I had many unsolvable and unanswered questions. What was the issue that caused such vicious acts of violence? How could I prevent myself from being in this situation? What were the preventable signs, if any?

Sadly, I would see similar stories on the news, and the killer's neighbors would attest that he was such a nice person. I never admitted these thoughts to any of my partners, but I used extensive cognitive resources, wondering if they had the potential to be a killer. I drove myself crazy and assumed a ready-to-fight mentality if any of my subconscious signals appeared.

One of my previous partners was passionate about the poem The .38 by Ted Joans. I supported his desire to create a film based on that work because I believed he would be a great filmmaker. However, I despised the concept but repressed my true feelings. I was not honest and courageous enough to object to the high level of domestic violence. Instead, I subconsciously wondered how such a poem could be a source of inspiration to anyone.

That was then, I recently reread the poem, and I now agree that it is very vivid and powerful writing. Choose your character and imagine your next; any which way, it's a tragic end. Ironically, I now interpret the poem with new light and new eyes. The details seem to align with my now brave attempt to normalize the idea of death. Nonetheless, my childhood experiences made me wonder about the storyline and if it could become my reality.

I was ten years old, attending Titchfield High School, when a full market truck veered off the road and down the gully, killing multiple passengers. One of the passengers was my friend's stepdad, and another was a female student from our school. While in the 10th grade at St. Catherine High, another classmate died in a car accident. He was with us on Friday and never returned to school on Monday. At that young age, my soul still believed that our world was beautiful. Other than discussions about the ozone layer and pollution, life was simple. Life was good.

I must also mention Tino, whose death was a shock to me. I wrote this book to prevent others from saying, "I can't believe he or she died." Yet still, I cannot believe Tino died so senselessly. I knew him briefly and mostly from afar as he would ride his bicycle past my home to and from wherever he had to go. He was such a brilliant, gentle soul. Who would have thought someone would have killed him on a visit from college in his hometown, where such acts were unexpected?

Death of A Star

I was on the 3rd floor of 15th Avenue School printing the 8th-grade yearbooks when the news announced Michael Jackson's death. I witnessed the world stop and mourn the loss of a talented artist. Even though I watched and listened to MJ all my life, his death was not as devastating as learning about the death of the late Airmiess Joseph Asghedom (Nipsey Hussle), an artist I barely knew.

I never listened to his music until around the time of his death. His song "Hussle and Motivate" caught my attention, and I found some of his interviews through YouTube recommendations. One of the first videos I watched was his controversial plans to create a Dr. Sebi documentary. I then saw an interview with him and his partner Lauren London. They seemed like a perfect match for each other. His level of enlightenment immediately caught my attention. I realized he was extraordinary from his music projects and business ventures.

After his death, I learned he taught himself how to build a computer as a child. His music, thoughts, philosophy, and lifestyle showed he had overcome so much to reach his high consciousness level. He focused on his purpose and became innovative and artistic. He desired wealth and abundance, and he served his community.

Coupled with Nipsey's upbringing in California, his dad took him to Africa to broaden his thinking. He learned the importance of integrity, confidence, and how to be a leader from his dad. On the other hand, my father was very busy traveling from one church to the next, while my mother sewed night and day. I could not go anywhere without my parents, so my life revolved around school and church. The lack of financial resources also helped confine my awareness. I was curious, cautious, and a lot naive. I learned to be kind and meek and the need to work extremely hard to survive.

Like much of the world, Nipsey's senseless murder on Sunday, March 31, 2019, still saddens me. My sister Bridgette and I recorded a video discussing his death one Sunday after church. My nephew Alwyn who studied video production at Rutgers University, created a professional video presentation. I may share it for this year's memorial.

Lack of money, like death, also promoted a feeling of doom and a mandatory sense of contentment. I desired so much but had to be happy with what my parents could afford. I would look at clothing magazines and envision wearing the clothes. I would also read a recipe book and imagine eating all the food and pastries. As an adult with the financial means, I still allowed myself to occupy that same limited bubble. I was progressing with imposter syndrome, being mentally satisfied with the photo of a recipe instead of enjoying a delicious three-course meal. I was unintendedly trapping my soul and desires into a mental casket.

While acknowledging and mourning those who had died, I simultaneously sought wisdom and understanding to release my full potential. Bishop TD Jakes's Sunday morning sermons and Wednesday night bible service significantly impacted my spiritual growth. Even today, his messages help me process my emotions, reflect on my situation, and internalize my stance with God.

The first memorable sermon I heard Bishop Jakes preach was These Are They, on May 27, 2012. In summary, your seed can be planted by the wayside, on rocky ground, amongst the thorns, or on good ground. A seed is a potential or possibility, like a tree in disguise. It has its value, but you cannot see its immediate worth. In time and with patience, if you protect the seed, you will see it grow to its full potential. God will do everything great in your life through a seed. Your fruits will be great if you can be faithful to the tiny seed. The tiny seed also represents the people we overlook because they lack materialistic resources. However, they may possess a divine internal power.

My journal entry for that date states that Bishop Jakes preached from St. Mark chapter four. He likened our spirituality to the word and the sower who planted his seeds in many places. The outcome is different for each planted seed based on the environment.

Those by the wayside get snatched away. Some never made it or stayed long enough on the ground before the birds representing the devil took control. Seeds planted on stony or rocky ground could not survive for long as the shallow environment did not allow for the deep penetration of roots. This is a spiritual example of a lack of commitment. Seeds often stifle when planted with thorns. They could not develop to their potential growth due to the world's richness or deceitfulness. Those grown on good ground could produce and multiply in folds of 30, 60, and 100. Am I planted on good ground?

The moral of the sermon is opportunity and potential combined with the right environment will result in measurable gains, not all equal but all equitable. God is an unfair and just God. He disseminates the right amount of struggles and success based on your spiritual capacity. All I could say was wow, upon rereading my writing.

In 2015, Bishop Jakes delivered a sermon titled "Blinded by Rage," which emphasized the importance of controlling and managing anger instead of suppressing it and warned against not addressing issues.

This was a direct message because I often avoided problems instead of dealing with them. He suggested that disrespect and emotional, verbal, or physical rage towards loved ones often stem from a lack of self-love. The sermon cited Ecclesiastes 7:9 and encouraged listeners to share God's goodness. The impact of the message was profound. Each insight has stacked up and led to this moment and completion of this book.

Both sermons provided literal and figurative insights into my life. I was trying to establish my roots on good ground while undergoing an internal rage for not meeting the expectations I created for myself on behalf of society. My guiding light knew I had a seed to plant, but I didn't know where or how.

I expressed my internal rage as sadness, disappointment, or irritability. I was preoccupied with busy work instead of value-added tasks. I told myself I needed to be involved, always show up for my children at school and events and take the lead at home. I told myself I needed to work late and at home to finish incomplete work projects. Who told me this? I told myself society expected me to acquire a school leader position after gaining my first and second advanced degrees. Again, who told me this? Society did not call or send me an email. I made it all up because I lacked love for myself and craved love from others. I did not have the confidence that Nipsey Hussle learned from his dad as a child.

While attending primary school in Jamaica, my class routinely recited, "labor for learning before you grow old, for learning is better than silver and gold; silver and gold will vanish away, but a good education will never decay." I must have committed that to memory because I now have three degrees with the possibility of a fourth. Likewise, my classmates and I would collectively say, "good, better, best, never let it rest until my good is better and my better is my best."

Both are great mantras to establish the importance of education and the need to work hard towards continuous improvements. However, I feel something is missing and misleading in the first one. Silver and gold are necessary. If used correctly or invested well, they will not vanish away. They can also provide the financial means to be a lifelong learner through academics and immersive life experiences like traveling.

In the past, I internalized death and the invisible thoughts and opinions of others. Unfortunately, this left me vulnerable to obsessively judging myself. The death-related scenarios I mentioned became ingrained in my subconscious and controlled me like a monstrous enslaver. Fear, combined with a lack of awareness and belief, created a life of misery and unproductiveness.

Bob Marley's Redemption Song has always been my favorite song, with its powerful message "emancipate yourself from mental slavery." It was as if I subconsciously knew I was living in my mental slavery while also being mentally enslaved by someone else.

I now acknowledge and release my fear of death. In addition, I now realize that my neutral, diplomatic personality is my innate desire for peace. I am confident that I value peace and freedom. I urge you to release your fears and identify your core values. Release all negative thoughts and influences. While you cannot predict the unexpected, you can prepare for them with persistence, an internal drive, and a positive mindset. Let's now get beyond your fears.

And deliver them who through fear of death were all their lifetime subject to bondage.

Hebrews 2:15 (KJV)

CHAPTER 6

GETTING BEYOND MY FEARS

Traveling by motor vehicle or public transportation became a nightmare. In the seventh grade at Titchfield High School, a non-cancerous tumor developed behind my right eye. I had terrible headaches and couldn't see the blackboard after a while. I traveled from Port Antonio to Kingston to see Dr. Shaw, the Ear, Nose & Throat specialist. I underwent surgery to remove the tumor and spent about two weeks in the hospital. Imagine a little country girl in the heart of Kingston surrounded by strangers and making the best of a dire situation.

I would also visit my sister Maxine in Kingston and later in Spanish Town during the holidays. Occasionally, I would even travel by bus for church trips across the island. Traveling through Junction was the most stressful of all the roads. It was hazardous, narrow, windy, and hilly. You could see the gullies below lined with trees, wild bushes, mountainous rocks, and often a stream or river from the vehicle. As a child, my thoughts would race, and my heart would palpitate until I reached my destination and returned home. Junction connected Portland, St. Mary, and St. Andrew, leading to Kingston.

Vendors, including my dad, used public transportation to travel back and forth from Kingston Coronation Market. Most of the buses that transported passengers also transported them and their goods. The drivers would pack the top of the bus with bags of ground provisions from bananas, yams, coconuts, vegetables, fruits, and sugarcane. Occasionally, a bus or truck would overturn and kill some passengers.

Hence, I feared traveling on those country buses to Kingston and back home to Port Antonio. No wonder my dear Papa would talk about Jesus on the bus and shout loud hallelujahs with special and unique sound effects. He, too, must have recognized the risk of our travel. He was trying to get others to give their lives to Jesus and connect directly with the higher being for traveling grace and mercy.

Years later, multiple airplane crashes made a bad thing worse. You guessed it; these experiences limited my interest in traveling. I would love to see the world, but that would require me to drive, fly, or sail to the location. Instead, I would have been quite happy staying home. The possibility of death while traveling outweighed the gratification from the experiences. So I have chosen to stay still. Yet, I don't think that was the intention when God said in Psalm 46:10, "be still and know that I am God." I did have one moment of courage, thanks to my ex-husband for planning our three-week vacation to Japan in 2005. That's the farthest I've traveled and the only destination I've visited outside Jamaica.

Further ingraining my fear of death and travel was the crucifixion movie at the age of ten. I was very disturbed by the lack of respect and reverence for Jesus. He had given his all to his community, completed many good deeds, and improved people's lives. He fed the hungry and healed the sick but was rejected and sacrificed. I wondered how they could choose Barabbas, the sinner, over Jesus.

How could those in power falsely accuse and charge Jesus, who only had good intentions? Why would popularity be used as the basis of decision-making instead of evidence and sound principles? But we know how the story ends; all things worked for good. Christ had to be crucified to save us from our sins. Even though the crucifixion was the ultimate goal, I was traumatized that a person could possess the qualities of a good human being yet be wrongfully incarcerated or killed.

The movie and the above experiences created a sense of doom in my spirit. I recognized the need to serve God, so at ten years old, I pledged to become a Christian when I turned thirteen. I wanted to "live life a little" before surrendering to God. How did that turn out for me?

Thirty-four years later, I did not honor my commitment to myself, and I am reminded of it every year that I get older. I also have not lived the life filled with joy and happiness that I envisioned as a child. I live a Christian-like life; however, I have not committed to a church or been baptized. Nonetheless, there is no doubt that my newfound relationship with God has made me stronger and happier than ever before. Yet, fear still tries to consume my life.

My recent revelation is that some church has possibly caused more harm than good. So many children start in the church, leave the church for personal reasons, and eventually return as adults after severe tribulations and enlightenment. The primary issue is that some preachers focused on an all-or-nothing, damnation-filled, poverty approach, which caused many to stray. Once in the world, distractions, temptations, and acts of sin in the pursuit of joy often result in increased hurt and heartache. Some of these are a natural part of life, as discussed in the chapter on embracing the darkness.

The church should encourage its members to establish a deeper relationship with God and self instead of casting judgment and shame on its members. In connecting with God and myself, I have found a genuine, internal joy instead of a perpetual search for imaginary pleasure. Thankfully, some churches provide members empowerment and self-improvement resources as they seek God's abundance.

I recognize that God is within us, and loving God means first loving ourselves. The next step is treating oneself like God treated all sinners with kindness and mercy. If we treat ourselves with compassion and understanding, we will only partake in activities that will benefit and not harm us. That starts with the things we feed our minds, the food we put into our mouths, and the actions we inflict on our physical bodies.

The same notion remains true: if we love God and ourselves, we will wholeheartedly love and respect others. With all my faults, thoughts, and indecisiveness, I know there is a God who has protected me, provided for me, and has great plans for my future. Therefore, I understand and empathize with the faults I experience in others. I digress in discussing God, but I now reside in his presence.

Throughout my life, I created a massive, uncontrollable narrative on how to prevent my death. My natural mental action was to be very fearful and suspicious of everyone. It didn't help that I had a very active and imaginative mind. I decided that I couldn't trust friends and possibly family, I couldn't trust the uncertainties of life, I couldn't trust my lover or spouse, nor could I trust strangers or public transportation. Limiting my travel was a strategy to reduce the likelihood of getting into an accident. How about unfair punishment? Since Christ was punished for doing good, I needed to be an extraordinarily 'good girl' to keep the boat steady and prevent unfair judgment.

How did I transition to a place of peace and being at peace, even when faced with conflicts? First, I consult God on all things because I have set a track record of not always making the best decisions. I read books and listened to wise and successful people. I focused on value-added thoughts. I strategized, innovated, and imagined a life of abundance and joy. I realized the need for a personal improvement system to address all areas of my life. I reflected on one of my Seton Hall University courses where the professor, Dr. Mitchell, taught about the importance of being happy and fulfilled educational leaders.

I also incorporated a few life lessons with my information systems (IS) decision-making skills. Information systems is the strategic use of people, processes, and technology in the form of hardware, software, and data for decision-making and competitive advantage. My undergraduate degree is a Bachelor of Arts in information systems from Rutgers University and New Jersey Institute of Technology (NJIT). As an adjunct professor at NJIT since 2015, I taught the Introduction to IS course for several years.

Data is the fundamental component of IS. Most organizations combine data to create information and gain knowledge. Ideally, the outcome is wisdom. Students in my class learned how data is captured, stored in a database, and retrieved for analysis and reporting. The information systems process requires a network for data transmission and policies to address privacy and confidentiality. Lastly, data security and visualization are also critical. That said, please use strong passwords and two factor authentication to secure your data.

Information Systems use decision-making tools to determine trends and make projections strategically. Examples of tools are a pro/con list, a SWOT analysis, and decision trees. According to ChatGTP, decision trees are hierarchical structures representing a sequence of decisions and their consequences. They are used to classify data into different categories or to predict outcomes. A decision tree is one of the methods used in artificial intelligence (AI).

Information systems surround our daily lives, from finance, medicine, and agriculture to transportation. You use IS to make informed decisions when you extract or exchange information via an app, online form, website, or private portal. IS includes electronic transactional systems such as online banking and orders, checking the weather, watching movies on your SMART TV, or logging on to your doctor's patient portal. As a juror, I was astonished by the legal and forensic information systems used in the courtroom.

My fears and indecisiveness often ignored sound decision-making principles, like the ones I taught my students. To improve my life, I needed to practice what I professed. I implemented a system that could help me move from inaction to action, from fear to fierceness, and from idea to results. I called the system my A.R.A.D.A.R. framework.

The first step begins with ACCEPTANCE, moving to REFLECTION, AWARENESS, DECISION, ACTION, and ending with the desired RESULT. With every thought, idea, or goal, I first accept my current state, then reflect on my life to better understand the impact of my past actions on my quality of life. I then explore all my viable options and resources to increase my awareness. I needed to make decisions and step forward regardless of distractions or possible downfalls. I have also learned that simply acting is insufficient; I need to work in a result-oriented direction. In the end, I evaluate and celebrate my results.

As you think about your fears, loss, or aspirations, give yourself the authority to accept your situation. There is no blame or regret, just acceptance. Next, reflect on past actions to understand what caused specific results to avoid repeating them. It may require you to forgive yourself or others for where you are.

On the contrary, you can also show gratitude to yourself or those who contributed to your journey. Now with your GPS set, become aware of all your possible routes, and decide on the one that is best for you. You then act, knowing that hiccups, stop signs, roadblocks, and obstacles are inescapable. With your goal in mind, be committed and persistent, seek help, and create partnerships, but do not stop until you obtain the desired result.

To become something, you must know your starting point and be okay with it. It doesn't matter if you are not where society expects you to be physically, mentally, professionally, spiritually, or financially. You must love and appreciate yourself in your current place. With this sense of gratefulness, you can eventually master life's challenges to achieve your goals and get to your higher ultimate self.

Sadly, I am just exploring my untreated emotional hurt. I was moderately depressed, went through therapy, and was prescribed medication, but a fear of death was never discussed or identified as the root cause of my many issues. I did not realize death was an unconscious concern until I started writing this book. How could I not see that my actions correlated with my past experiences of loss? The fear of death is a self-made belief system I allowed to keep me captive.

Your perspective of death may be based on close encounters or local events that created an impressionable thought in your subconscious. Likewise, your journey may be much more severe or not as bad as the moments I encountered. No two experiences are the same, and experiences should not be compared. It is the emotional impact that matters. How did it make you feel, what thoughts occurred, what were your actions, and are you proud of the results? Lastly, what changes can you make to get to the goal or the vision of yourself that you seek?

I am just connecting the dots. My natural mental actions have been to live protected and crippled in my fear of death. Ironically, it seems to constantly be with me for something I've tried to avoid. I have held and cuddled it all my life. I must release those thoughts and misguided stories to be at peace with myself and the world. Today, I pledge to live a free and abundant life because my ultimate self depends on me to do so. Join me in part two as I learn to accept and be at peace with the death of a few close friends and family members.

PART TWO

Accepting death as a natural part of life. Each person was born to die ultimately. At the time of death, each embodies the best and worst of who they could be in this lifetime.

Both birth and death coexist on opposite ends of the spectrum. A balanced mix of negative and positive actions in the middle creates the destined versions of ourselves at the time of death.

During loss, we become our most authentic, vulnerable selves. We yearn for less grief and the return of joy. If only for a moment, we act kindly, remember to be grateful for life, and reside in a place of hopefulness.

I pay tribute to four special people and share how death became my motivator.

Therefore we are buried with him by baptism into death: that like as Christ was raised up from the dead by the glory of the Father, even so we also should walk in newness of life.

Romans 6:4 (KJV)

CHAPTER 7

DEATH OF A PARENT

Reginald Birch was a fierce and committed man of God. He was born to Hadlyn Manning and Lorenzo Birch in 1923. He had a difficult life with his mother passing away when he was only four years old. Eventually, he felt compelled to serve God at the First Holiness Church of the Apostolic Faith in Swift River and across Jamaica. He remained connected with his non-saint friends to bring them closer to God. He loved cultivating his land in New Eden, Swift River, and sharing his ground provisions. Most of it he gave away or sold at the most reasonable price. He knew all the bus operators who transported goods from Portland to Kingston. He was a carpenter and tradesman, overseeing the building of roads, bridges, homes, and buildings. When my mom, Bridgette, and I migrated, he decided to stay in Jamaica. Later, he wanted to travel to the USA, but the process became complicated.

He had friends in high and low places. Before I migrated to the United States, he wanted to introduce me to his friend, an administrator at Mico Teachers College. He regularly visited parts of Kingston where non-residents needed prior authorization before they entered; he asked no questions. He feared no one, worked hard, and asked for what he wanted. So, what on earth happened to me? What caused my overwhelming fear and lack of urgency to act? Why don't I claim the abundance that is rightfully mine despite all my years of education, career dedication, and community service?

He taught me to embrace masculinity through lessons on mixing mortar, laying bricks, using a level, and removing a nail with a hammer. We discussed the moon cycle and reviewed the farmers' calendar to determine the best time to plant crops. His hallelujahs were so untimed and resonating that they would scare me. I used to be so embarrassed when we traveled together that I asked him not to shout hallelujah on one of our trips. How dare me? He did it anyway. I learned my lesson; as sure as the bus would stop, my dad would release a few hallelujahs and even preach a long enough sermon. I just had to get used to it.

Imagine being on the bus in the 1990s, before the innovation of ride-share apps, Walkman, AirPods, or Beats headphones. You have no choice but to listen or exit the bus and wait a few hours for the next one to arrive. Or take the challenge and walk to your destination.

My father possessed a compassionate heart, particularly for children. He would give away his last dollar to ensure a child could afford transportation to and from school or purchase lunch. I am confident of this because he would utilize the money Bridgette and I gave him to assist members of his community. Although it was exasperating because he still had personal expenses to fulfill, we had to resend the funds, hoping he would not give them away again. So technically, Bridgette and I have funded lives and dreams through our dad.

The passing of family members is a recurring theme in my life. Most of them died due to natural causes and old age. However, my grandfather's death remains painful because someone poisoned him. Since then, I have experienced the loss of my grandmother Irene Williams, formerly Cooper. She was like a dainty doll who served her ten children, grandchildren, and great-grandchildren until she passed in her nineties. There were uncles, aunts, great-aunts, great-uncles, and cousins. The passing of these loved ones has been a challenging experience, but none compared to the immense pain I felt when my father died.

I still remember the Tuesday afternoon on October 8, 2013 when my sister Bridgette walked into my office on the third floor of Ivy Hill School and said that our dad had died. I told myself it couldn't be because I had just spoken to him on Saturday. He was his normal self. As usual, he asked about everyone, including Alyssa, Ethan, my now ex-husband, and Sister Birch, my mom. As always, he prayed for my sister Bridgette and I. Unknowing that it would have been our last phone call, I recorded our conversation from my MacBook Pro. I was creating screencasts on how to use PowerTeacher, so I just pressed record while we talked. I still have difficulty listening to the conversation. My intuition to record our conversation, and other moments throughout my life, prove that God has a divine connection with me. As such, it will always be okay, even in my darkest hour.

My dad's passing evoked unimaginable emotions. He was 90 years old, but I thought he had more time. At least enough time for me to go back and see him. It had already been over a year since I saw him in 2012. Looking back, I prioritized other things, projects, and people over him. What do you do when different aspects of your family demand your attention? It is heart-wrenching to find yourself in a place where you feel obligated to care for everyone and mostly everything. If you are at the stage of starting a family, I encourage you to seek relationships that promote partnership, empathy, and a strong belief in God. A lack of these can forge neglect and regret.

Going to Jamaica to see my dad for a weekend was not an easy decision to make. I felt compelled to be at home to take care of my two young children. I valued my family, connection, and helping others, so the thought of leaving my young children behind evoked guilt. Not to mention taking time off from work, PTA obligations, or pausing my New Leaders leadership studies. Combining my fear of dying by airplane made it easy to fuel that narrative and not travel to Jamaica. I cannot blame my ex-husband because if I felt an urgency to travel, I would have strongly communicated my desire and found the most convenient time to go and see my dad. Yet, I now see how I developed unconscious resentment and transmitted that guilt to my ex-husband, especially after my dad died.

That said, I sense that my dad died of a broken heart. It could be accurate, but he knew the time was nearing, and he desperately wanted Bridgette and I to visit him. I am learning to forgive myself if that is the case. I also need to release that story because it may not be valid. My dad probably died because God decided it was his time. Who am I to create my narrative about God's intentions?

I can easily make this story because I identify with wanting to be loved and seen. I have yearned for appreciation and the need to feel whole. Comparing the polarity of the emotions of abandonment to being loved and cherished, I realize that the former makes you want to give up on life, while the latter gives you a sense of will and reason to live.

In the past, I yearned for love and acceptance to validate my presence and existence. I now know that my core values create the confidence and certainty I need in all areas of my life. I have also recognized a difference between physical and spiritual sight. The physical eyes can be judgmental and approach life from a position of lack. Some people will judge you based on their experience and expectations. Like the half-empty glass, you will be assessed based on your inadequacies instead of your assets and potential. A person who sees beyond your physical realm coats your actions with acceptance and a growth mindset. There is an understanding that each person is born for continuous improvement. As such, you are loved for who you are and there is pure joy in the idea of who you can become.

For years, I felt someone out there had the love and affection I needed. Simultaneously, my dad would tell me to give my life to the Lord. It wasn't until recently that I realized that the someone I sought after was the Almighty God that my earthly father spoke of tirelessly. I should have listened more keenly to those sermons on the bus. I now know that true love comes from within and from God.

Just as I resorted inwards after multiple experiences of loss, I now lean inwards, seeking to nurture, console, and encourage my inner being. The eternal love and affection that I seek must first appear within. I cannot hold someone else accountable for loving me if I do not first love myself. With internal maturity, external appreciation becomes unnecessary but is still accepted with sincere gratitude if it occurs. Like my earthly father, I am about my heavenly father's business. He alone has the credibility to promise and reward a life of abundance for living purposefully and serving others.

The duality of life became prominent after my father's death. Life can seem complex, but it is simple. God created multiple subsystems within a system. There is nothing more significant than a system. For example, our universe operates as a system. The earth rotates systematically, similar to how we breathe systemically. These systems accommodate the diverse range of human inconsistencies in a structured manner without mass chaos.

Life operates in a natural cycle of birth and death, active and inactivity. The birth of my first child involved positive energy, light, movements, and joy. My dad's death created emotions on the opposite and negative end of the emotional spectrum - the darkness, the hurt, and the place of stillness and eternal rest. A newborn enters this world through pain, but the immense joy overshadows those feelings. Our loved ones die, and sometimes they create tremendous hurt and pain. One commonality between both events is that both emotions last but only for a while.

The initial sadness that I felt after my dad died would often interrupt my daily thoughts and actions. It would appear unexpectedly and suddenly. Time does heal all wounds, physically and emotionally.

Time does not promise to eliminate the hurt, but you eventually get to a place where you can process it sensibly and controllably.

Thanks to my dad, I have an affinity for my elders and their wisdom. My dad, the late Elder Birch, constantly reminds me to be a good person. I try, but please understand that I am still human. I embrace being a loner, charting my path, and attracting the people who align with my energy. I also understand the plight of the working class and effortlessly recognize the struggles of individuals seeking to achieve their higher purpose. I pray that he helps me navigate my indecisions and bad decisions. I want him to know I made his name proud and will forever be Elder Birch's daughter. Happy 100th Heavenly Birthday in May 2023!

Let me not see the death of the child. And she sat over against him, and lift up her voice, and wept.

Genesis 21:16 (KJV)

CHAPTER 8

LOSING MY GRANDNEPHEW

I did not see this coming, and nothing could have prepared me for my grandnephew's death. Javanie Cox was born on August 18, 2002, to the parents of Saskie Bell, my niece, and Marvin Cox. My sister Sharon is his grandmother. He was eighteen and filled with life, aspirations, goals, and ambition. He loved his family and friends and was a light to everyone he encountered. He attended school in Jamaica before migrating to the United States. His last two high schools were Irvington High and Hillside High, where he graduated with immense pride in July 2020. He was an avid soccer star and always represented Jamaica in his personality and personal accessories.

Sometimes, it feels like it's my first time learning this news. I was always proud to call him my grandnephew. I traveled to Jamaica in 2002 when he was born at Port Antonio Hospital. In later years, he, Alyssa, and Ethan would hang out when my family visited Jamaica. When he came to the United States, I was happy that he finally arrived and that my children now had an older cousin they could interact with and model.

I felt a sense of joy when I learned that he was studying Computer Science at Kean University because it aligned with my goal of making technology accessible to all students. I taught teachers how to integrate technology in the classroom for years and worked with my technology club students. I also led K-12 Computer Science Education for the New Jersey Department of Education and facilitated stakeholder meetings at Kean University.

He completed his first semester on December 17, 2020, and died a few hours later. Once again, Bridgette, my sister, was the bearer of bad news. She called me about 5:00 a.m. on December 18, 2020, my 15th wedding anniversary, to inform me that Javanie had died in a car accident. I was stunned, numb, and hurt. He had just finished a shift at Amazon and was driving home on the Garden State Parkway North. His vehicle veered off the road at exit 138, hit the first tree, and he died.

It was a hectic week as he completed finals and maintained his work schedule. Bridgette saw him the Monday before he passed. He wasn't thrilled about his grades, and knowing the over-achiever that he is, we're almost sure he was working tirelessly to improve his final grades for the semester.

The frustrating thing is my family does not know what caused him to exit the roadway. There is one speculation that he fell asleep. It could be that he was trying to avoid hitting another driver. Another possibility is that the previous day's snowstorm could have produced enough residue to create black ice on the road. Undoubtedly, this latter scenario blossomed into fear. Immediately after his death, my anxiety increased if I had to drive in the snow or during a rainstorm. Since then, I've relaxed my emotions but proceeded with heightened caution, especially on the Parkway. The highway authorities recently cut down the tree that Javanie's vehicle collided with. Even without a marker, each time I drive north, I remember that is the spot where Javanie took his last breath. That is where he became the ultimate version of himself.

We have so many what-ifs. One thing is for sure; he will never return to us in the physical realm. Another thing for sure is that I felt a deep, unnerving hurt I had never felt before. It was close to the feelings I experienced when my dad passed but more intense. During this season, I also went through the agonies of divorce mediation. This new emotion was beyond my hurt on my worst mediation day. I immediately released my ego. I had to forget about myself while simultaneously recognizing the importance of my being. How could I continue to focus on feeling unworthy, heartbroken, and victimized when I have life and the ability to change my circumstance? My grandnephew no longer had those options.

The loss of any young, promising soul is a tough thing to accept and process. It is even more overwhelming when it is your grandnephew or a close family member. I have not mastered the journey, but I have gotten to a place of peace and acceptance. It is one of the reasons I decided to write about my journey and experience with death.

I try to remember the last moments we had together. I attended Javanie's high school graduation in July. He was so proud as he stepped wearing his red cap and gown to collect his diploma. He drove to Brick, New Jersey, where my sister Maxine held her 60th birthday party. I was so surprised that he was now such a good driver. About a month later, he stopped by my new apartment to give me a bracelet his mom, Saskie, had made. We talked outside on the porch about whether his dad would buy him a car for Christmas. I also wondered what gift to get him now that he was a working adult. The most memorable moment was his act of randomly visiting my mom, his great-grandmother. My heart melted when I visited her, and he came to check on her.

So, on Friday, December 18th, I took a personal day off from work and forced myself to take a lead position. I called his college to inform them about his death. I later created his funeral program, designed his website, organized the zoom meeting, and attended the funeral on December 28th. When you are in battle, action is required. You have no choice but to perform, looking fierce or falling apart.

Over the years, I have mastered this public performance of playing life instead of living my truth. I would be hurting inside but trying hard to keep it together on the outside. Then reality sets in during my moments of solitude, and my mind, heart, and soul get wrapped in impressionable footprints. There is no resolution than to fall to my knees and beckon God.

How do you get through those private moments of battling the pain of losing your loved one? From my experience, you must give yourself the authority to process your emotions, if only for a moment. Depending on where you are, pause and take a few seconds to acknowledge your feelings. I often say, "Javanie is no longer here." I then mentally or verbally say, "it is okay; I recognize your presence, now, let's move on; let's get it together." Next, proceed to revisit your internal database of highlight reels of the person. Extract a happy moment that will pull you out of the sadness.

My memory of Javanie was his smile, a video of him at work telling his co-worker to "smile for the gram," his comedic t-Shirts, or his holiday reindeer outfit that he wore to my house to collect his 2019 Christmas gift. Those and other moments kept me going during the initial difficult times. Create your database of happy memories. Keep them ready and accessible to help you navigate your emotional journey.

Going through the emotions, I wondered how I would face significant milestones such as visiting his graveside for the first time or celebrating his birthday. Surprisingly, returning to his graveside took me a while, but it was not as bad as I had imagined. Six months later, on a sunny June morning, I walked into the cemetery and was at peace. I should not have taken that long to face my fears. Another lesson proved that our fears are often nonexistent or not as terrible as we imagine.

One positive outcome of Javanie's death is the realization that the end can come unannounced, and you must accept, embrace, and prepare for it. This experience has given me a renewed way of looking at life and realizing the need to work towards becoming the best version of myself. I have since been on a journey to establish who I am and who God wants me to become. I am developing my cause and call to action. I plan to achieve it in Javanie's name and my dad's.

Remaining optimistic, inspired, and seeing the good in everything, every action, and everyone. If you have experienced a similar journey, I encourage you to achieve your goals or commit to finishing the work your loved one started.

His lord said unto him, Well done, thou good and faithful servant: thou hast been faithful over a few things, I will make thee ruler over many things: enter thou into the joy of thy lord.

Matthew 25:21 (KJV)

CHAPTER 9

A COMMUNITY SERVICE PARTNER

Marcella Oglesby was a high-energy, friendly, and outspoken individual. She was a school Social Worker, wife, mother, and community service member who died of cancer several years ago. Her purpose was to help children process the trauma they experienced in their personal lives and from tragedies in their communities. As a result, she created Pathways to Healing, an organization to support grieving students.

We met as members of the Zonta Club of Essex County. She enlisted me to provide technical support for her organization. I would have helped her for free, but she was adamant about paying me for my service. She recognized my expertise and was willing to compensate me, even when I did not value what I had to offer. For that, I thank her.

Sadly, I did not understand the importance of her work and the reason for her passion. That's even after creating the Facebook account for her organization, designing the conference brochure on normalizing loss, and creating the name tags for speakers. I finally realized the relevancy of her work when my grandnephew died, and my soul cried out for direction.

I saw my entire family grieving; we all needed to be comforted simultaneously and at different times. Javanie's parents - Saskie and Marvin, his grandparents, aunts, uncles, baby sister, cousins, my children, his friends, and even former teachers were deeply saddened by the tragedy. Why did it take this long to recognize the importance of Marcella's work? As I navigated my emotions, I felt compelled to create something aligned with her purpose.

I still remember her visiting my former house and taking my daughter walking around the block. She was highly involved in Zonta's scholarship program, which provided funds to graduating female high school students in Newark. She was unafraid to talk loudly, be authentic, and dance at our Zonta jazz functions. The last function she attended was the summer Jazz brunch at Society Hill in Newark. She had a great time dancing and entertaining our guests.

Even due to her prior illness, her death was still unexpected. I was shocked when she passed because she seemed to have been recovering well. I remembered her a week ago when I attended the Newark Legends awards event. My spirit led me to console a mom whose fifteen-year-old daughter died from gun violence. My thoughts went back to my grandnephew Javanie and Marcella. I sympathized, but I dear not claim to know how she felt. I didn't share her relationship with her daughter, their journey, and their love. However, I understand the possible hurt and emotions that stirred and vibrated deep inside.

I remembered Marcella because she would have supported any program that promoted grief relief and normalizing loss, both related but very different. This book is a tribute to her legacy, aimed at helping people move beyond the initial shock of losing a loved one.

Even as I strive to understand death more deeply, I still struggle to accept that Marcella is no longer here with us. No strategy will ever fully erase the disbelief and pain of losing a loved one. Still, hopefully, my journey can provide you with comfort, ease the grieving process and help to normalize the reality of death.

Jesus said unto her, I am the resurrection, and the life: he that believeth in me, though he were dead, yet shall he live.

John 11:25 (KJV)

CHAPTER 10

DEATH OF A FORMER CO-WORKER

Wakina Humphrey, aka Leopard Phresh, was full of energy and passion. She was a dance teacher, a single mother, and an entrepreneur who lived her truth. On the evening of April 12, 2022, I had been worshiping alongside Kari Jobe's song The Blessing. Crying at my bedside, I thanked God for his work in my life and family. I envisioned his goodness in my future years. Seeing my children's children become the ultimate version of myself and my vision. Then I heard the news of her passing. My tears of joy and gratitude became tears of hurt and sadness.

We worked at Fifteenth Avenue School and Ivy Hill Elementary School in Newark for years. She was the dance teacher while I was the technology coordinator. As such, we spent much time supporting students' visual arts performances. Spring and winter concerts, Black History Month celebrations, Alvin Ailey's dance residency, and graduation routines were yearly events. I am honored to have the recordings from the Wiz production to students dancing to Beyonce's I Woke Up Like This.

I was also the school testing coordinator, managing all district and state tests, such as the former PARCC and NJASK assessments. She always made herself available to be a test administrator during testing. Our sons spent a year in the same PreK3 class and shared a few birthday parties and special outings. She supported Bridgette's Jamaican restaurant and spoke highly of my cooking, especially my mac and cheese.

My heart sank when I heard the news. It was the same hollow, shocked feeling I felt when I heard about my grandnephew and my dad's death. Unlike Marcella, who I previously mentioned had died from cancer, Wakina's death was so unexpected. She wasn't feeling well and eventually went to the hospital, where she later died.

Expected loss hurts, but your mind, body, and soul get to process the reality before life's finality. Unexpected and sudden loss does something to the psyche that shocks and stresses our system. The thought of life just ending without notice proves our fragility and creates the awareness that we, too, could die suddenly. Therefore, this uncertainty of life should form and solidify our common humanity and propel our greatness. Likewise, the question what if I die today helps to reduce the severity of that suddenness.

At Wakina's funeral service, the presiding pastor's message was to make each day count. It gave me a new sense of purpose. The celebration of life ceremony highlighted the importance of living YOUR life. You must show up daily being the person who resides at your core. Only you can be you. You cannot live someone else's life, and someone else surely isn't going to live your life for you. So, be yourself, uninhibited, with your greatness and your flaws. Love, embrace, worship, dance, speak your mind, and express your desires and frustrations. Be as God expects you to be - good to yourself and one another and living in his likeness.

In this Easter season, I realized that death is inevitable, whether expected or not. So each of us has to reach a mental place of accepting that death will outlast the best of us. Like the inevitability of the crucifixion, we must acknowledge that it can and will happen, even to me. Therefore, be ready for it, prepare, and plan for it. Other than buying life insurance, death requires mental and physical preparation.

I felt at peace when Wakina's mom sang during the service, and her son spoke highly of his mom and his love for God. Proving that weeping may endure for a night, but joy cometh in the morning. "For his anger endureth but a moment; in his favour is life: weeping may endure for a night, but joy cometh in the morning" (Psalm 30:5).

So, with life's challenges, we will be hurt for a while, but joy will surely come again until we depart this earth. Therefore, I encourage you to condition your mind to live on that promise. Make your life count, and never miss an opportunity to dance or be kind.

Dancing and worshiping are two ways to express our emotions. Whether hurt or grateful, I release all inhibitions and embrace my inner self on the dance floor. Wakina taught students how to master this process. So, dance if you are dancing, and love if you love. Whatever you do, always be your best. Not knowing if it's your last step or action, make it count and leave a lasting positive impact.

And the Lord answered me, and said, Write the vision, and make it plain upon tables, that he may run that readeth it. For the vision is yet for an appointed time, but at the end it shall speak, and not lie: though it tarry, wait for it; because it will surely come, it will not tarry.

Habakkuk 2:2-3 (KJV)

CHAPTER 11

DEATH AS MY MOTIVATOR

In 2015, I felt I had the potential to obtain opportunities to prove my worthiness and share my talent with the world. I had all the ingredients of someone who could do much more but couldn't see how to get them done. I got involved in various activities and programs thinking I was serving others, but instead, I was out-serving myself.

I was married for almost ten years and a mom of a nine-year-old and a seven-year-old. I was working in my twelfth year as a School Technology Coordinator. I was a Teachers College, Columbia University graduate and working on a second post-graduate degree from Seton Hall University. As a registered business owner, I also had marketable skills to share. I continued to learn and serve. I became a Google Certified Trainer. I was the Tuscan PTA Secretary, an Adjunct Professor at NJIT, and the City of Newark Caribbean Commissioner. Seriously, just trying to remember all this makes me exhausted!

They were not all intentional positions or experiences. Without a goal or plan, I sometimes allowed myself to become immersed in new roles, ideas, possibilities, or other people's dreams and visions. Ultimately, I appreciate every opportunity for the knowledge gained, however insignificant or impactful.

I needed guidance, so I enlisted a mentor, Mr. Don Viapree. During the first meeting, my assignment was to make a list of my fears and a list of aspirations. My next task was to visually and mentally overcome my fears. For each, I needed to determine the source of the fear and identify the common sources. I had to envision the fear happening, how I would deal with it when it happened, while it was happening, and after it happened. Since death was my number one fear, I prioritized it first. Visualizing being dead was extremely difficult, especially after my dad's funeral in 2013. However, it was a life-changing, cathartic exercise that I encourage you to complete.

This activity may be like a few educational philosophies, such as backward design or beginning with the end in mind. Imagine yourself in your casket at your funeral. Create a holistic mental image of the surroundings but do not get caught up with the intricacies of the physical environment. For example, don't focus on the color of the casket; the types of flowers; is your best friend in attendance; who is late as usual; or whether there are grammatical errors on the program. However, from my perspective, errors are different.

I see myself shaking my head in my casket if there are program errors. It doesn't matter at that point, but I would still be bothered by misplaced or missing punctuation marks. God forbid, don't leave the 'h' out of my name. Not to mention images inappropriately aligned or not having the correct dimensions and aspect ratio. Please, no excessively stretched images. But seriously, now that I'm thinking about it, I think I should create the program and share the editable Google or Canva link so there is no confusion when I die.

I digress, but you should remain focused. Your current thoughts should be on the atmosphere, who is in the room or wishes they could be in the room, the life you lived, and the lasting impact of your legacy. Imagining myself in my casket below the preacher motivated several life-changing decisions over the last eight years. Feeling stuck, unappreciated, and destined for death, I fully completed the exercise. I was moved to tears as I visualized my death. What would be my story, how would I have lived, and who would I have helped? Did I enjoy life, or was it filled with hurt and insecurity? My answer was that there was a conflict between my life and my spirit's vision. If I had died, I would have been an educationally accomplished, hard-working, unhappy, and unfulfilled person.

Immediately, I knew I needed to change the narrative to one where I felt at peace with the time God allowed me to live on earth. I needed to create the happiness that I desired. I needed to focus, value, and develop myself. I needed to help others in tangible ways, similar to my dad.

As it happens, God sent me a revelation. I may have misinterpreted this message, but I started to imagine joy and love and eventually manifested this experience in my life. I began to love Esther. Unfortunately, this change was temporary. I was still yearning for

79

external gratification and appreciation from others. Over time, other personal and professional issues brought me to my knees, and I once again questioned my commitment to self and God.

It is now eight years later, and I am almost at the point of figuring out the steps I need to take to become the person I envision. My entire journey is for another book at a later time. The key idea is that accepting who I needed to be at my death was the kickstart to finding, becoming, and acting like the person I need to be now.

Your ultimate self can be a version of yourself in six months or at a significant milestone. The vision of your ultimate self at death may change as awareness, choices, innovations, opportunities, and socio-economic needs change. You have the power to decide. Just be motivated and act.

PART THREE

Clarity is recognizing and owning the light that is within you.

Understand and believe that "you have favor," which means your next is already in you. It is already done.

Master yourself and connect with the higher being. Seek and collaboratively create your guide to align with your expected outcome, your ultimate self.

Fear none of those things which thou shalt suffer: behold, the devil shall cast some of you into prison, that ye may be tried; and ye shall have tribulation ten days: be thou faithful unto death, and I will give thee a crown of life.

Revelation 2:10 (KJV)

CHAPTER 12

QUANTUM ENTANGLEMENT

I may have mentioned this before, but Brené Brown, as a guest on OWN's Soul to Soul, said that something has to die for something to live. It made perfect sense. For your aspirations to thrive, your fears must end. To see in the dark, you must shine your light. To gain clarity, you must seek knowledge. To run a marathon, you must make incremental or quantum steps, starting with the first one.

To successfully adapt and grow, it is necessary to venture beyond one's initial place of comfort and shift focus. This involves changing one's perspective and exploring new environments until the unfamiliar becomes comfortable. Letting go of desires that do not serve this goal.

You are probably wondering what quantum entanglement is and how it relates to this book. Separating from my ex-husband meant leaving the 2018 Audi Q5 behind and using my 2003 Honda Accord. It was well-maintained, with less than 100,000 miles. After listening to Bob Proctor in 2020, I decided on a goal to buy a safe, comfortable luxury SUV.

I hadn't driven my Honda for a while, so I spent about two thousand dollars to make it inspection ready. This decision seemed like a good idea before minor issues became inconvenient problems. There were hot days when the air conditioner didn't work and cold days when the heat stopped working. Over time, the windows didn't work, and the steering wheel became stiff because the rack and pinion had to be changed.

When my mechanic had to work on the car, I would rent a vehicle from Enterprise, borrow my sister and niece's car, and even take public transportation. Taking the bus to work reminded me of traveling between Orange and Newark on the 21, 24, and 44 buses while attending Rutgers and NJIT. Only this time, I was sad and stressed, yet hopeful. It was a challenging time. An appalling experience was the passenger who sat beside me and started to shave his beard and hair. I had to excuse myself from my seat immediately.

I soon noticed a familiar theme of holding on to things that no longer served me. It was time to let go of the Honda and move on. If not for myself, my children, Alyssa and Ethan, deserved a safer vehicle. Therefore, after months of researching and test-driving vehicles, I was excited to purchase my 2022 Range Rover Velar.

At a stop light in Newark, I pulled down my window and acknowledged a gentleman wearing a hat with the word God boldly written on the front. Surprisingly, he then asked if I had ever heard about quantum entanglement. I told him no. I knew quantum computing, the quantum leap TV series, but Professor Lewars didn't know about quantum entanglement. He handed me his card, and I went home and researched the term. I have yet to connect with him, but I appreciate the enlightenment from such a random encounter.

According to Wikipedia, quantum entanglement is a physics theory where knowing the state of one particle immediately creates knowledge of the opposite and connected particles, regardless of the distance between them. An analogy is when a coin flips to the head, and the opposite side is undoubtedly the tail. Likewise, if it is nighttime at your location, it must be daytime on the opposite side of the earth.

Similarly, scientists can predict the current state of a distant particle based on the state of its connected, entangled particle. It is a physics phenomenon that I will continue to research. Based on the academic inclination of Alyssa and Ethan, they will study these concepts and teach me more about them in the future.

Imagine observing a stone causing ripples in the water. Likewise, consider that our actions and emotions generate waves of varying magnitudes. The region near the source would experience stronger waves, whereas the ripples would weaken as they travel farther away. Concerns affecting our families tend to carry more weight, whereas external issues may capture our attention but do not elicit the same degree of emotional investment or care.

During my quantum entanglement research, I came across quantum mechanics waves and how difficult it is to predict the exact location of an atom. However, scientists can indicate the possible path where you will find the particle. I then realized that human beings are just the same. First, life happens in a series of waves - ups, and downs. Then, no one can predict every microsecond of their entire life. There are, however, possible paths and intentions that you can achieve.

Several years ago, I was diagnosed with Mitral Valve Prolapse (MVP), a prevalent heart condition characterized by valves that fail to close correctly. Every one or two years, I visit the cardiologist and complete an echocardiogram to monitor my heart's condition. Each time, the test results serve as a reminder of life's fragility and beauty.

The heart, responsible for sustaining our existence, operates in a series of peaks and valleys. A healthy heart displays consistent waves and a flawless rhythm. Like the changing seasons or our day-night cycle, our heart functions as a constant system. Medical professionals identify irregularities in heart function when wave patterns become disrupted or exhibit excessively high or low peaks.

So, expect life experiences to be a series of peaks and valleys with levels of depth. However, imbalance occurs when you stop, veer off your path, and stay too high or low longer than usual. Ungratefulness, narcissism, egotism, jealousy, low self-esteem, and depression reside at these extreme destinations. As you inhale and exhale, move eagerly yet humbly with your rhythm.

In extrapolating the meaning of this stop-light encounter, I concluded that we are all connected as human beings. It reaffirmed my mentor's advice to recognize the reason behind every biological interaction. Every human stare or glance may hold a secret message from our past or future. Every chance encounter is a calculated path to our destiny. I've also deduced that, like a yawn, or a ripple, our emotional states transcend and play an essential role in relationships.

The energy we emit directly influences others. It creates similar cascading effects on the people around us, especially our loved ones. For example, if a person is miserable, the prediction is that their spouse and children will also be miserable or sad. If a person is happy, those around them will show the same energy or at least be inspired to be happy.

There was a saying growing up in Jamaica, show me your company, and I will tell you who you are. That is, you are a product of your environment. It's not impossible, but it takes resilience and mental strength to be part of a community and not exhibit similar behaviors. Therefore, manage your energy field to gain the happiness, joy, and success you seek.

Please excuse my repetitiveness; death is inevitable, and one thing must die for another to live. What are the things that you need to eliminate in your life? What are the cycles that need to break? Of those, which ones are you willing to permanently kill so that you can live to your fullest potential? I prefer to kill all inadequacies, doubt, fear, negative influences, and harmful habits. Their impact and outcome have been detrimental to my success and purpose. So, commit to their elimination and pursue the known, opposite reaction.

Flow with the wave of life; expect and appreciate the lows as much as the highs. Although joy should constantly be present, it is often not the case. There are moments when my greatest joy is expressed through solemn tears in solitude, as I reflect and be grateful for my life and loved ones. Likewise, when the highs come, celebrate but don't stop. Keep riding your wave to your ultimate destination, creating positive quantum entanglements and leaps throughout your life.

In all labour there is profit: but the talk of the lips tendeth only to penury.

Proverbs 14:23 (KJV)

CHAPTER 13

TAKING RESULT-ORIENTED ACTIONS

I prefer to stay home and hide from society's demands, evilness, and injustices. If you have ever had those same thoughts, unfortunately, that's not always feasible, and it is not the recommended way to live a fruitful life. We must live, work, and associate with others. We must establish connections and develop meaningful, lasting relationships. We must also develop programs and strategies to navigate disruptions and provide solace for others.

The lingering thoughts of regrets and inaction must overpower the fear of death, which can impede a person's purpose and potential. You must believe that you have favor with God, so fear nothing. As philosopher Osho stated, go blindly into the unknown without a destination or map; just have the desire to discover. It is best to clear your mind of all negative thoughts and believe that God will lead the way.

Before writing this book, I regretted not visiting my father in Jamaica before he died. I regret not communicating more with my grandnephew. I could have encouraged him to take it easy, not work so hard, and instead focus on college. I could have visited Marcella before she passed or scheduled a time to meet up with Wakina.

At the beginning of the 2021-2022 school year, I saw Wakina briefly outside Ivy Hill School, and she asked me if she would see me inside. Due to the district's COVID-19 restrictions, I didn't enter the school building. There are so many things that I could have changed. You can probably relate to my journey and have reflected on acts you could have done differently.

In October 2022, I purchased a Self Concept one-on-one coaching program. It is a Neuro-Linguistic Programming (NLP) method focused on updating your database to include your certain values and qualities. After all the obtained education, self-education, sermons, and online influencer videos, my soul was still yearning for a missing component. Pavlok, my accountability partner, recommended Self Concept, and I immediately saw how it would help me reconnect my thoughts and past actions to my intentions and future self.

It was a worthwhile action and investment that will help me in my work, personal life, and business. This experience allowed me to mentally revisit my missed opportunities to determine my positive intent and give myself the necessary resources to improve the situation. Don't just meditate on the past or things you no longer have control over.

I also realized that I needed to accept the current state of my life. Take responsibility because the movie called life was rendered and finalized without an edit button. The only possible change is to update the credits to include your plans. The question you must ask is, what are the things that you must focus on now? What must you do to improve yourself and make your loved ones proud? Who do you need to check on? Which relationships need to be rebuilt? What new partnerships can you explore?

After asking these questions, make a realistic plan that you will follow. Next, execute your plan and remain persistent until you achieve your desired goals. So start the project, make the call, send the text, or take the trip. Do one or do them all, but please do something. At this point, I must mention one of my favorite books: The Science of Getting Rich by W. D. Wattles. He states that equivalent riches will come based on your definiteness of vision, the focus of purpose, the steadiness of faith, and the depth of gratitude. In this sense, riches are financial but can also be anything you value and desire. Set your mind, heart, and hands to achieve your goals.

Committing to yourself and taking action will help to prevent future regrets when you reach the next crossroad of death. I commit to dreaming, doing, being, and having more. I plan to show up, speak, lead, innovate, create, connect, and contribute. Even in this current moment, there are things I could have done in my last moment. For example, you probably saw a friend's post about life being difficult. Did you just send a care emoji and keep scrolling to the next highlight reel, or did you pick up the phone and call that person?

I recommend returning to a communal society where we verbally and visually connect. A phone or video call may prove to someone that there is a reason to live, that they matter, and humanity still exists. So say hi to strangers, call a friend, and check on a loved one. It's not just for them; it's also for you. It's building a legacy of things you will be proud of when eternity arrives.

The exercise for this chapter will allow you to use my A.R.A.D.A.R. framework to help you select your next priorities. A.R.A.D.A.R. stands for ACCEPTANCE, REFLECTION, AWARENESS, DECISION, ACTION, and RESULT. It is a six-phase system to help individuals get past their implementation dilemmas. No more woe is me.

1. Acceptance: Accept your current situation. Take a picture or create a snapshot of your circumstance(s). Address one area or different areas of your life. At this point, it is what it is.

2. Reflection: Reflect on the problem or situation. Review past practices. What were the actions, and what were the outcomes? Forgive and show appreciation. What are your new goals and expectations?

3. Awareness: Research your options. Create awareness of what's possible. Find thought leaders and experts. Log and compare your findings to help with phase four.

4. Decision: Make a decision. I may speak for myself, but this can be a dreaded task. You must select one of the options from the awareness phase. It does not need to be the best decision but the most valued one for the issue, time, and circumstance. Decision-making tools such as a pro vs. cons list, SWOT analysis, or weighted decision tree can assist you in this process.

5. Action: Result-oriented implementation. Start and continue to make incremental steps toward your goal. Monitor your progress.

Make the changes that are necessary to propel you forward. Strategize, seek guidance, form partnerships, and develop a database of resources to support your growth. Whatever challenges occur, do not give up; please remain persistent.

6. Result: Based on the desired outcome. Congratulations. There is not much more to say. You have mastered yourself and your habits, and you have achieved the goal that you desired. Celebrate your success. Share your lessons learned. Move to your next plan.

After using and mastering this method, you can select any step as your starting point. In time, you will see results if you decide and act.

And it was so, when the king saw Esther the queen standing in the court, that she obtained favour in his sight.

Esther 5:2 (KJV)

CHAPTER 14

I HAVE FAVOR, AND SO DO YOU

With my sister and mom, I bought my first home at twenty-three years old. While married, I moved and lived in a beautiful, five-bedroom suburban house. There were more bathrooms than people in my house. I was overweight and unfocused. I had substantial student loans and credit card debt. I earned enough income to help maintain our family lifestyle. However, being comfortable, I had no urgency to use my expertise and entrepreneurial skills to invest or gain a higher income. I created Vernov Technology Group, LLC, over twelve years ago but did not promote it. When pursuing leadership opportunities failed, I gave up too quickly and questioned my worth, decisions, and faith in God.

God has continued to bless and provide for my children and family. I endured situations and experiences that are best left unsaid. I survived my darkest moments using various resources and strategies. His goodness brought me out of my days of depression, fear, grief, and self-doubt. That same goodness makes me grateful for life and gives me the faith to believe that abundance and impact are imminent.

Today I call that goodness favor. Writing this book is my first act of urgency and a demonstration that I must not just survive on God's goodness. I must produce, serve, and create opportunities for myself, my family, and my community. I must immediately plan and execute because my biological clock is counting down with every passing second. I must use the favor he has bestowed on me since I was in my mother's womb.

When my faith wavers, I remember three events where God displayed favor: my first car ride to the hospital, my eye surgery, and Queen Esther in the Bible. I remember my mother speaking about the day she went into labor with me. Standing by the roadside with her packed bags, a good Samaritan, a Caucasian male, stopped and gave her a ride to the hospital. I was born that night. She did not know the driver and had never seen him again. She would have gotten to the hospital eventually, but God provided for her and me in a time of need.

Another example of his favor was when the doctor successfully removed a non-cancerous, growing tumor from behind my right eye at ten years old. With a bulging eye and sharp headaches, surgery was a necessary risk. Over thirty years later, it had to be God's goodness and favor where I only had a minor scar, and my sight was unaffected.

Now to my name - Esther Elizabeth Birch. As a child, I did not like the double dose of elderly first and middle names. People called me Easter, Ether, or I had to ensure it was spelled Esther, not Ester. I now appreciate the power and favor associated with both, especially Esther.

She found favor in the King's sight, as evident when he said unto her, "what is thy petition? and it shall be granted thee: and what is thy request? even to the half of the kingdom it shall be performed" (Esther 5:6). Let's just say that at almost 45 years old, I have my list of petitions and requests. I will know I have found my king as soon as I hear those questions. I now love and identify with Queen Esther, a woman positioned with favor for a time like this.

Going through illnesses, financial debt, depression, divorce, and the death of my loved ones has given me the evidence and reason to bask in and appreciate God's favor. I am also realistic in knowing that having favor is a great start, but it takes more to make progress. You must act in your favor. In Luke 1:30, the angel approached Mary and said, "fear not, Mary: for thou hast found favour with God" not too long after, "Mary arose in those days, and went into the hill country with haste." She was disturbed, but she did not stay still and became depressed. She had courage, got up, and sought counsel or company. She moved from her current environment to another.

Therefore, while death can motivate us to become the best version of ourselves, we can also rely on God's favor. He has given us a gift or talent to accept, nurture, and birth. Though it may be challenging to take responsibility, we must do all necessary to bring it forth and release it into the world. We must seek the required resources or mentorship and be willing to move physically, mentally, or spiritually.

So act now in your favor. Seek the knowledge, resources, and guidance you need to move from fear to faith or from loss to hope. Seek joy, peace, and contentment. You have favor, so embrace it and fear not.

Delight thyself also in the Lord: and he shall give thee the desires of thine heart.

Psalm 37:4 (KJV)

CHAPTER 15
HABITS I USED TO WIN

Jesus said unto her, I am the resurrection, and the life: he that believeth in me, though he were dead, yet shall he live: and whosoever liveth and believeth in me shall never die. Believest thou this? (John 11:25-26 KJV)

First, believe that you deserve positive habits. Our habits have a powerful impact on our lives, whether we realize it or not. From the moment we wake up to the moment we fall asleep, we engage in habits that can either support or hinder our progress toward achieving our goals. These goals can be as small as waking up at 5:30 am every morning or stopping for pedestrians while driving.

For many years, I struggled with discipline and consistency. Despite my enthusiasm for starting new projects or pursuing new goals, I often needed more momentum and gave up when faced with obstacles or setbacks. Looking back, I realized I needed routines and systems to help me implement my plans effectively. I enjoyed learning, leading, and sharing ideas but shied away from taking responsibility and blamed my failures on being overwhelmed or lacking resources. In truth, my fear of failure and inner doubts fueled my complacency. I also forgot to be grateful for God's blessings and favor.

But everything changed when I discovered the power of habits. I learned I could progress toward my goals despite challenges by developing small, consistent habits. In this chapter, I want to share the habits that helped me succeed in various areas of my life, including my career, finances, health, and personal growth.

Over the past three years, I have used my experiences of loss to rediscover myself. I realized every setback, accident, broken promise, or failure had a life lesson to teach me. I learned to embrace my mistakes and see them as opportunities for growth and learning. You must reconcile what you perceive as a failure with your positive intentions.

On July 4, 2021, alone in my apartment, I reflected on the Think and Grow Rich movie I had just seen on YouTube the night before. I realized that my ultimate goal was to obtain freedom. It was one of the reasons I decided to walk away from my marriage and home in 2020. However, this time, I didn't just want freedom from my ex-husband. I wanted mental freedom, financial freedom, freedom from health issues, freedom from work constraints, and the freedom to be my authentic self.

I sought joy and developed a relationship with myself and God. Doing so allowed me to overcome the pain of losing my loved ones. I finally understood the meaning of life and death. It helped me accept better the news that another soul has departed. It also prepared me to deal with future hurt and loss. I must state that this is not a place of being fearful and guarded but a place of enlightenment, acceptance, and peace.

When I have a problem, I pray and ask God for a solution. He often provides the answer through the universe. As part of my daily routine, I remain grateful for everything, even the mishaps. I curate songs that inspire my soul and even give answers to my questions. From Fantasia's Lose to Win and Chronixx's Thanks and Praise. Most recently, Tasha Cobb Leonard and Popcaan were at the top of my playlist. Tasha sings Gracefully Broken and This Is a Move, while Popcaan's God Alone is a testament that I now rely only on God. His accord ordains my human partnerships and interactions.

I listened to motivational speakers like Les Brown and the late Bob Proctor. I used my local library's online audio resources. I read books such as As a Man Thinketh, Think and Grow Rich, The Science of Getting Rich, and Can't Hurt Me, to name a few. I still listen to Bishop TD Jakes and his daughter Sarah Jakes Roberts. I join mastermind groups such as the Persistent challenge and attend alum meetups and professional meetings.

For sustained communities, I joined online challenges such as Tony Robbins and Dean Graziozi's Project Next and the Self Education Revolution community. Touré Roberts The Called to Pioneer and Bishop TD Jakes Woman Though Art Loose virtual conferences were like spiritual supplements. I must also mention Myron Golden, who teaches prosperity using evidence from the Bible. He led me to The Path to Prosperity challenge and conference, which opened my eyes to new wealth concepts. At that conference, I saw master speaker Dr. Dellatoro who leads the Monetize Your Message challenge and Crush the Stage program. He taught strategies on how to become a successful professional speaker.

I attended face-to-face conferences such as Woman Evolve 2021 in Texas. My spirit and soul exhaled at Woman Evolve. A new life was born after hearing Pastor Sarah Jakes Roberts (SJR) preach. Thanks to her and Self Concept coaching, I plan to host a women's conference in New Jersey.

Exercising was never a priority. I now make it a habit to walk for at least an hour in my local park every weekend. During my walk, I photograph nature and connect with the environment. At the beginning of each chapter is a photo from my walking routine. I now also have an active gym membership. Working out and using the sauna, steam room, and hot tub are priceless resources that improve my mental and spiritual well-being.

I am proud of my nutritional changes, resulting in a weight loss of thirty pounds. Give and take a few standard deviations depending on the season. Taking on the task of reading the bible in its entirety, I came across Genesis 1:30 - "behold, I have given you every herb bearing seed, which is upon the face of all the earth, and every tree, in the which is the fruit of a tree yielding seed; to you it shall be for meat." Why was I just seeing this? God gave specific instructions about what we should eat. He did not include curry goat, oxtails, or the infamous Boston Jerk Pork. I now use the Jamaica Health Box herbal products. They consist of detox, blood cleansers, and supplements. Some are very bitter, and it takes mental resilience to open the bottle, much less swallow two to four tablespoons daily.

I reduced my carbohydrate intake and opted for healthier options such as mushrooms and spinach. My typical lunch is a salad with chickpeas and other toppings. I select salmon over steak but will partake if offered. I reduced my alcohol intake but must keep my Jamaican white rum on hand. If I weren't me, I would not recognize the person drinking kombucha instead of a Jamaican ginger beer.

I have moments of weakness and allow myself to indulge without guilt. That includes the occasional snickers or kit-kat from the receptionist desk, the glass of wine, or a delicious cupcake at the office birthday parties. In all things, it's about acting with moderation and always remembering that your body is a holy temple, so treat and respect it accordingly. If I genuinely love myself, I will only ingest things that benefit me and not cause harm.

I made a personal decision to stop taking my depression medication. I kept the last prescription bottle of Sertraline, also known as Zoloft, to remind me of the days I needed it to perform. Seeking therapy well into 2021 allowed me to process feelings related to losing Javanie, my divorce, and work discomfort. One piece of advice from my therapist was to do more things I enjoyed doing. So, I found opportunities to dance, walk more, and photograph nature.

My children are now my cause and reason to develop new habits. God has blessed me with a fruitful womb. Alyssa and Ethan are exemplars of reasonable human beings. Both are hardworking, talented, academically gifted, have great sportsmanship, respectful and ambitious. You would think there isn't much more to do, but I realize that my insights are necessary to give them a level of understanding that will make them mentally strong. That's the God-designed task for my life.

In all that I do, I try to be a role model for them. In 2014, I started wearing my hair naturally so that Alyssa could identify as a strong, confident black girl in a diverse school community. I decided to change our family dynamics so they could see their mom as a strong, confident black woman. I pour love, light, and power into them so they can see and direct their beam.

Other impactful interactions include that with my accountability partner Pavlok. He also seeks a higher version of himself, thus providing constructive feedback on each other's goals. We share resources and brainstorm ideas in our Thrive Accountability Group.

Separating from my spouse forced me to take control of my finances. I no longer passively contributed 50% of my income toward home expenses. I was now responsible for it all. As a previous homeowner, this was a familiar yet different process. It was the height of COVID-19 with so much uncertainty and emotional trauma.

After reading Secrets of the Millionaire Mind by T. Harv Eker, I divided my net income to meet the suggested guideline. The author suggested using 50% for necessity and the other 50% divided into five categories. Those categories are (i) give, (ii) education, (iii) play, (iv) long-term goals, and (v) financial freedom. I only budget 2% of my income to help others, and my necessities are well over 50%. My formula is different, but I have been consistent. I even use my ex-husband's advice to automatically transfer the amounts from my checking into individual savings accounts. This strategy gave me a sense of assurance. I was now saving and could effortlessly manage unexpected expenses.

CashApp and Zelle allow me to easily use my 2% to show appreciation to a hardworking student or support a struggling friend or family. I share my network and connect individuals to needed tools and resources. I enjoy helping since God has always provided for me.

On July 5, 2021, I committed to a 30-day ab challenge. I completed 15 crunches, a 10-second plank, and six leg lifts on day one. Each day the crunches and the planks increased by five, while the leg lifts increased by two. I was consistent for several days, then missed a day, sometimes several days. I did not stop; I kept going. Initially, holding a plank for 30 seconds was difficult, but by October, I easily completed a 155-seconds plank, 64 leg lifts, and 120 crunches in one setting. I did not follow the standard consecutive 30-day routine, but I continued to challenge myself until the end.

After my dad died, I questioned God, the church, and the people in the church. I remember staying away from church for a while. No one knew that my absence was intentional. I was hurt to see that my dad gave his entire life to his church and died a lonely pauper. That was a wrong perspective and interpretation.

My new peace and joy made me realize that my dad probably had this same peace and understanding. He always encouraged me to give my life to the Lord. That is why he asked me to buy a microphone and speaker system so that he could preach in the streets. That is why he habitually encouraged others to find God. He did it through the church but not for the church. He did it for the people, his purpose, and God.

Therefore, I shouldn't be upset because he acted based on his enlightenment. He felt compelled to share his journey and joy with others. If he returned to this earth, he would still preach and encourage people to give their lives to God. I now must follow my dad's path of helping people attain internal joy and experience everlasting peace.

It was not my intention to still be writing. There will be other opportunities to share my journey, but I want to provide an excellent start to understand that the pain from your loss is normal. There is a community of individuals who may share your exact circumstance. If interested, you can use the available internet tools and social media to find local support groups.

Find the resources that speak to your specific needs. Try new activities and consistently repeat positive steps until they become second nature. Positive routines, habits, and consistency build confidence and belief in ourselves as we prove our persistence and get things done.

Overcoming the fear of death and the grief related to loss is essential to move on to the next stage of yourself and your life. Accepting where you are and committing to change is the first step to progress. Wherever you start, implementation is where life begins. You must get to that place of action to feel fulfilled and proud that you can continue in and for your loved ones who are no longer here.

Implementation can be gradual, over time, or immediate. My cognitive computing class at Teachers College, Columbia University, showed how to express each task as a list of manageable steps. Taking on a challenge or new goal can be overwhelming, so break it down into simplified steps. Systematically address each; you will have completed the entire process before you know it.

Today, I have no credit card debt. My student loans are a work in progress. I lost 30 pounds. I drive a comfortable, luxury vehicle. I monitor my health. I am mindful of what I eat and take time to exercise. My spirit and mind are stronger than ever. I have new goals and desires, such as buying a new home, exploring speaking opportunities, and investing in real estate and people. Most of all, I wish immaculate health and prosperity for all I encounter.

Reviewing the TD Jakes sermons I have watched, I came across one of his first recordings, Breaking the Cycle. He confirms my sentiments that everything produces after its kind. In addition, everything operates in cycles. Lastly, I am already blessed, so when problems persist, we must break the issues for our blessings to return and flourish. Likewise, for habits to thrive, we must break any existing cycle and work diligently towards our goals.

I encourage you to set goals and routinely reward yourself for your accomplishments. Be kind and loving to yourself as you navigate through this process. If you fail, don't give up, just continue or start over. You owe it not only to yourself and God but to your loved ones, those deceased, those here with us, and those in the future who will benefit from your thoughts and actions today.

Become the person you'll be proud of when your time comes to rest. Remember to travel with knowledge, grace, strength, and humility. Embrace the journey, as it is the most critical part. Act boldly, and achieve great things, starting with one habit at a time.

For this God is our God for ever and ever: he will be our guide
even unto death.

Psalm 48:14 (KJV)

CHAPTER 16

RETIREMENT AND LAST WILL

The White Ash tree in the picture to the right has been alive for 340 years. It has seen over 124,000 sunrises and outlived some brilliant minds. It endured many scorching days and frigid winter storms. As such, I revere it each time I visit the park. I connect with it for the wisdom it possesses.

I embrace the strength and longevity of the white ash while accepting that extended life is not promised. Living to my dad's or maternal grandmother's age would be great. Likewise, preparing for my death will require more than a mental resonance. Both require putting things in place and organizing the assets I will leave behind. As such, this chapter provides practical advice for preparing for a stress-free retirement and your death.

There are several ways to invest for retirement, and the best approach will depend on your financial situation, risk tolerance, and retirement goals. Below are retirement options to explore. Research each and contact a financial advisor for expert advice.

Employer-Sponsored Retirement Plan 401(k) or 403(b): Many employers offer retirement savings plans, such as 401(k)s or similar accounts, where you can contribute a percentage of your salary to a tax-advantaged retirement account. Your employer may also offer matching contributions up to a certain amount. As an educator, I have a 403(b) as my retirement option. I have been contributing to this plan since I started as an educator.

Individual Retirement Account (IRA): An IRA is a tax-advantaged account you can set up independently with a bank, brokerage, or other financial institution. You can contribute up to a certain amount each year, and the funds can be invested in various ways, such as stocks, bonds, and mutual funds. A similar option is a Roth IRA which offers tax-free growth and tax-free withdrawals in retirement. With a Roth IRA, you contribute after-tax dollars, and your contributions grow tax-free. You can withdraw your contributions at any time without penalty or taxes, and after age 59 1/2, you can withdraw both contributions and earnings tax-free. There are income limits for contributing to a Roth IRA, and contribution limits are currently $6000.00 per year. A Roth IRA can be a robust retirement savings and tax planning tool.

Stocks and Bonds: Investing in individual stocks or bonds can be a way to build wealth over time, but it's essential to understand the risks involved. Stocks and bonds can be volatile, and there is no guarantee of a return on your investment.

Real Estate: Investing in real estate can provide an income stream in retirement through rental income or property sales. However, owning and managing property can be time-consuming and require high upfront costs. My first home was a two-family house in Irvington that my sister and I still own. I learned how to be a homeowner and landlord. My children were born in this house, so I also learned how to be a mother. Though a one-family is more convenient, I recommend purchasing a multifamily home as an investment.

Annuities: An annuity is a contract with an insurance company that provides a guaranteed income stream in retirement. Annuities can be structured differently and may offer tax advantages, but they also come with fees and other costs.

Savings: If you are not interested in any of the above investment options, save a percentage of your income for your desired retirement lifestyle. This will help to supplement your pension or social security payments.

It's important to remember that investing involves risk, and there is no guarantee of a return on your investment. It's also a good idea to consult with a financial advisor to determine the best approach for you.

Preparing for death is a deeply personal process that depends on your beliefs, values, and experiences. Like the ARADAR framework, this process involves reflection and decision-making. Take time to reflect on your life, your experiences, and the lessons you've learned. Consider what matters most and what you want your legacy to be. During your reflection, note your digital accounts and plan to delegate access. Review your existing financial accounts and update the beneficiary information. Below is a list of recommended steps and general suggestions.

Ensure that your legal and financial affairs are in order. Create or update your will, designate a power of attorney, and plan your funeral or memorial service.

Communicate with loved ones. Share your wishes and plans with them and discuss death and dying openly. Everyone will be on the same page and can provide comfort and support for each other.

Seek spiritual or emotional support. Consider seeking support from a religious leader, counselor, or support group to help process your emotions and find peace.

Live life to the fullest; it's the reason we are implementing these strategies. While preparing for death, it's vital to continue living life to the fullest. Spend time doing things you enjoy and making memories with loved ones. It's the memories and connections that will make this process easier.

Death is a natural part of life, and while it may be challenging to think about or discuss, preparing for it can bring peace and comfort. Of the above suggestions, planning and organizing your legal and financial affairs is crucial.

Create a will, a legal document outlining how you plan to distribute your assets and property after death. I never thought I had enough assets to make a will, but I now understand the need for one. God has been good to me, so I must continue to show gratitude even in my death. I must acknowledge even the most minor blessing and plan for it after leaving. As such, I recently started creating a will. Your loved ones will need to follow the directives in your will, providing it was created using the expected guidelines and there are no legal issues.

Regardless of your assets, you should consult a lawyer. There are online will creation services and downloadable templates. If time is of the essence, write out the details on a sheet of paper and sign it with your witnesses. While the specifics may vary depending on jurisdiction and individual circumstances, a basic template for a will typically includes the following sections:

- o Introduction: This section identifies the person creating the will (the testator) and confirms their intention to make a will.
- o Executor: This section names the person responsible for managing the testator's estate and carrying out the instructions outlined in the will. This person is known as the executor or personal representative.
- o Beneficiaries: This section lists the people or organizations receiving the testator's property and assets.
- o Assets: This section identifies the specific assets and property the testator leaves to their beneficiaries.
- o Guardianship: If the testator has minor children, this section will name a guardian responsible for their care if the parents die.
- o Funeral arrangements: This section outlines the testator's wishes for their funeral or memorial service. Do you wish to be buried in a specific location or do you want to be cremated? This is one example of a decision that will assist your loved ones as they arrange your funeral service.

o Signature and witnesses: The will must be signed by the testator and witnessed by two or more people who are not beneficiaries or the executor. This validates the will and confirms your wishes.

Despite having a will, some issues can develop. A will must meet specific legal requirements to be valid. It may be considered invalid and not legally binding if it does not meet these requirements. It can create confusion or disputes among beneficiaries if it is ambiguous or has an ambiguous language. Also, make sure that there are enough assets for all beneficiaries.

Remember that family members or other interested parties can contest the will if they feel they need to be adequately provided for or believe it is invalid. Be sure to select an executor who can carry out their duties. If not, your beneficiaries may experience delays and complications in estate administration, which can be long.

A poorly drafted will can have unintended tax consequences, such as increasing the estate's tax liability or reducing the inheritance beneficiaries receive. A will may become outdated or inadequate if there are significant changes in the testator's circumstances, such as the birth of a child, divorce, or remarriage. I advise you to plan and consult with a reputable attorney who can advise you based on your needs, assets, and liabilities. Yes, liabilities.

When you die, your liabilities, such as debts and outstanding bills, are typically paid off using the assets from your estate. The executor of your estate will first use the assets to pay off any outstanding debts and bills, such as mortgages, car loans, credit card debts, and medical bills.

If there are not enough assets to pay off all the debts, then the estate may have to be liquidated and the proceeds distributed to the creditors according to state law. Once all debts and bills have been settled, any remaining assets will be distributed to your heirs in accordance with your will or state law.

It is important to note that some types of liabilities, such as joint debts, may be the responsibility of the co-signer or joint account holder after your death. Additionally, certain types of assets, such as life insurance policies and retirement accounts, may pass directly to designated beneficiaries outside of the probate process and may not be subject to creditors' claims.

There is no indicator to predict our health or how long we will live during retirement. However, implementing value-added habits and lifestyle changes can improve our overall well-being and quality of life. From observation, those living a stress-free retirement were proactive in implementing systems and processes in advance. It is never too early or too late to start planning for retirement and your death.

I share this information, but please note that I still must organize my affairs. I need to solidify and be more aggressive with my retirement contributions, explore investment options, and finalize my will. I commit to implementing these strategies so that my retirement will be smooth, and my loved ones will have a guide to grant my last wishes. I am pleased when I think about creating generational wealth for my family. Contributing to ongoing philanthropic initiatives after I die is a legacy that will keep my ancestors and me alive. Their names will permanently attach to my history and my deeds. What will be your legacy?

I have been young, and now I am old; yet have I not seen the righteous forsaken, nor his seed begging bread.

Psalm 37:25 (KJV)

CHAPTER 17

BEREAVEMENT

I did not have the time to stop and process my dad's death. Since he was in Jamaica, there was a lot of uncertainty and remote planning. The entire family traveled to Jamaica on Sunday, October 20, 2013. So, my allotted bereavement days were exhausted somewhere between the airport and visiting the morgue to see my dad's still body.

Upon returning home, I went to work, continued caring for my children, and attended my new leader's professional classes. These movements were necessary because otherwise, sadness and depression could have set in. However, I realized that society and places of employment need to provide more time, space, and support for people to heal. Just as schools offer individualized learning, and insurance companies sell customized plans, there should be personalized bereavement because every situation differs.

No one should suffer in silence or delay their trauma until after work. I was showing up at work looking whole but broken inside. Self-control is necessary, but I shouldn't have to notify my brain to cease all sad emotions until after a meeting or presentation. There should be a normalized culture of support and understanding concerning bereavement.

I send special love and prayers to my niece Saskie Bell and my adopted nephew Marvin Cox, both parents of Javanie Cox. Thanks for bringing Javanie into this world to be a light before he transitioned from this realm. I know it has been challenging, and I love you both. To the Hillside High School soccer coaches, thank you for establishing the Javanie Cox Most Valuable Player Award earlier this year. I plan to establish a fund to support high school students who play sports, are from the Caribbean, or has interest in Computer Science, Information Systems, Agriculture or any skilled training program.

I will now acknowledge some souls who passed on after Javanie's death. In Florida, towards the end of 2021, my cousin Christopher was shot and abandoned on the side of the highway. His killer is still unknown. Granville Roberts, also known as Uncle Son, was my grandmother's first cousin who lived in the Bronx, New York. Crystal Stokes was a Newark Board of Education (NBOE) Human Resources benefits coordinator who helped me with my Family Medical Leave Application in 2018 and 2019.

Walter V. Genuario was my vice principal at 15th Avenue school twenty-one years ago. He served the school system for over 53 years. Retired Technology Coordinator Stacey Kim had an energetic and infectious personality. Having watched the reality TV show Braxton Family Values for years, I was shocked to learn that Tracy Braxton had died. I felt a sense of familiarity with the Braxtons, especially since both of our families have five daughters.

At a local nail salon in Irvington, Alexis Trusty invited me to stop by the Shani Baraka Women's Resource Center - I never made it. Like Shani, she is no longer with us. There have been countless family members of my friends who passed away.

From the news, the world mourned the loss of Stephen 'tWitch' Boss, a well-loved dancer. Tyree Nichols died from police brutality. Domestic violence took the lives of New Jersey educators Temara King and Luz Hernandez. Justyna Nieroda and her two children experienced a similar fate. Lastly, Elan Ganeles, a recent Columbia University graduate, was killed while visiting Israel. These tragedies are heart-rendering and remind me of my previous experiences and fears. May they rest in peace as they provide additional proof for the living to act urgently and make each day count.

To their families, know that they all lived an impactful life. I thank each person for their service and the joy they created during their earthly experiences. They now know and have an understanding we have yet to achieve. They became their ultimate selves.

For I know the thoughts that I think toward you, saith the Lord, thoughts of peace, and not of evil, to give you an expected end.

Jeremiah 29:11 (KJV)

CHAPTER 18

THE BENEDICTION

I was excited when my accountability partner 'Pavlok' proposed a 30-day book publishing challenge. It was the perfect motivation aligned with my recent writing attempt. Accepting the challenge seemed like an easy task. I had taken enough nature photos to pair with my favorite bible verses and inspirational messages to create a practical, low-content journal. After a few days, I realized I had more to share. The 30-day challenge became a six-month writing project.

I now understand why the writing process takes so long. With every intent to finish the book, I continued gaining additional inspiration and enlightenment on death. New knowledge continued to flow through my daily interactions with others and the world. I obtained value from attending church, praying, worshiping, or conversing with strangers. I now look forward to embracing opportunities that question my beliefs and mindset. I find satisfaction when creativity and innovation create a sense of certainty.

Watching Bishop TD Jakes's daughter Sarah Jakes Roberts excel as a humble servant motivates me to share my journey with others. She proved that being a young, black female who loved God and publicly acknowledged him was okay. She was authentic and even hilarious at times. I also observed how her husband Touré supported and loved her. I remember the first two videos I listened to while driving to and from Trenton in 2018. Make Your Bed and Embracing Your Legacy caused me to subscribe to her channel. I was hooked and transformed.

Sarah's YouTube videos were my light during my depression. They motivated me to become who I am today. Make Your Bed confirmed that God has great things in store for my life. I could relate to Embrace your Legacy because, like her, I lived my life trying to separate myself from the legacy of my parents being Christians and my dad being a committed minister. Again, I had to accept that, in the end, I would always be Elder Birch's daughter. Therefore, I needed to position myself to continue in that legacy.

I have since read Dr. Lisa Miller's The Awakened Brain, which explored a plethora of mental health data and scientific research on the impact of spirituality on brain development and depression. Without going into the details, I can attest that my spiritual awareness has improved my sense of self and purpose. I am confident that there is a God with whom I am deeply connected. I will emit his light.

Enrolling in Self Concept at the end of 2022 gave me new tools to transform and become my ultimate self. I discovered my values and certain qualities. I learned how to equip my past and future intentions with the necessary emotional resources. I cultivated a strong sense of certainty across all areas of my life. Imagine treating yourself with kindness and empathy even after you acted out of alignment with your values. Imagine using your available resources to better understand and associate with others, even when they aim to hurt you.

I give a special acknowledgment to my sister Bridgette. She took on the monumental task of editing my writing and providing feedback. If no one else reads this book, I am delighted you took the time to learn more about me. You may see me as a role model, but you, too, inspire me to act, live life, and become my best self.

My eldest sister Maxine has been my role model and is who I call my sister-mom. Sharon came to America and took advantage of all its opportunities. Her desire for knowledge, plants, and healthy eating habits makes me want to keep learning. Jackie is a communicator and community organizer. I admire her financial wisdom and hope to implement her spending restraints and money principles someday.

I am who I am because of my parents and ancestors. I will be all that I become because of them. To my ancestors, I thank you. Coincidentally I recently found out that I have the names of two of my great, great, great grandmothers. One was Esther, and the other was Elizabeth. Both were born in the 1840s.

My mother is my strength. She made me who I am, and I love her dearly. Like my dad, she helped those in need and worked hard to care for her children. She cared for my children when they were born and allowed me to continue working, learning, and serving. She constantly prays for all her offspring. As a Catholic, she encourages me to love Mary. I question my belief in that religion but acknowledge the need to honor our mothers. How can you love the son without loving his mom? Going forward, how a partner treats his mother or caregivers will be an indication of how he will treat me.

To my nieces, nephews, mother-in-law, and aunt Bernice, I love you all. Our love should be the model for all families. Aunt Bernice, none of this would be possible without your thoughtfulness to invite my mother, Bridgette, and me to migrate to the United States. I would not be here in this time and space if it were not for you.

My long-time friends Bernard Rollins and Keisha Jackson provide honest feedback. My new friends, Mrs. Amina Baraka and Alicia Graham encourage me to explore my past and enjoy the present. Charlette Jennings and Commissioner Reverend Ince always share words of encouragement. Juail Goode, thank you for investing in Vernov Technology Group services from its inception. Ms. Kettles, because of you, I started to create my will.

My mentor, Don Viapree, connects me to life's unseen frequencies and vibrations. LPR is my confidante who cannot wait to see me bloom. Conversations with these individuals create seeds of encouragement and enlightenment. I have no choice but to become the version of myself they have always seen in me.

My Newark Board of Education employment allowed me to serve students and the community for twenty-one years. I am grateful for the financial benefit, the joy of seeing my former students become adults, and the challenges I experienced that contributed to my growth.

My hometown in Maplewood provided the environment to write, improve my health, and explore nature. From sitting by the pond, walking in the park, or watching the miniature waterfalls flow without ceasing. I thank my ex-husband for selecting this town. Not only have my children thrived here, but I have also been honored to meet so many wonderful, talented, and authentic people.

The City of Newark Caribbean Commission has allowed me to serve my community and challenge my inner critic regarding public speaking. Eight years as a commissioner have opened my eyes to local government and formed lasting relationships.

Several years ago, my two-family house in Irvington was underwater. We owed more than what it was worth. In 2020, Bridgette and I realized that the housing market had changed. In my financial storm, a twenty-year investment provided the funds to pay down my debt and increase my credit score by 100 points. Sometimes we have everything we need internally and externally but disregard their importance. Sometimes old information is a detriment to our progress. We must keep up with current trends and monitor our assets.

I hope to one day have a strong knowledge of the Bible. Until then, I will continue to be inspired by chapters, verses, and stories that capture my heart and the essence of who we should be as human beings. There are a few chapters that were mandatory to learn as a child. Those include Our Father and The Lord is My Shepherd, Psalm 23 - "yea thou I walk through the value of the shadow of death I fear no evil." As I got older, I fell in love with Philippians 4:8, not the entire chapter, which I should probably learn in its entirety.

> Finally, brethren, whatsoever things are true, whatsoever things are honest, whatsoever things are just, whatsoever things are pure, whatsoever things are lovely, whatsoever things are of good report; if there be any virtue, and if there be any praise, think on these things.

Everyone should take this oath around age five. Yes, we are humans, have faults, and will make mistakes, but it should be our duty to think pure thoughts for ourselves and each other. Ultimately our thoughts manifest into actions. We can create the heaven we seek by managing our thoughts and promoting positive deeds.

Embracing our mortality can catalyze self-reflection, personal growth, and a deeper appreciation for life. We can live purposefully by releasing our fear of death, accepting our losses, and clarifying our intended purpose. We must create sustained habits, act toward our goals, and not let limiting beliefs hold us back. With determination and confidence, you can achieve. Remember, you have favor, so have faith, love yourself, and act according to your desires and light.

My latest inspiration is the song Not Afraid by Naomi Raine and Maverick City Music. It resonates with my achieved state of peace and being unafraid of death. W. S. Merwin's poem Thanks reminds me of 1 Thessalonians 5:18, which states, "in everything give thanks: for this is the will of God in Christ Jesus concerning you."

Be unafraid and grateful as you become your ultimate self. I thank you for your affection and support. Now, may the saving grace of our Lord and savior, rest, remains and abide with us now and forever. Amen.

RESOURCES

These exercises will help you analyze your experiences with death, stay on track toward your goals, and achieve your ultimate self. Each activity aligns with a specific chapter, but you can complete each independently.

Chapters one to four explored embracing the darkness, waiting on God, recognizing your light, and contemplating your mortality. Consider conducting a personal life audit first to get the most out of the exercises. Select at least six areas, such as emotional well-being, spirituality, physical health, finances, social life, and family, then create a snapshot of each. You should take a selfie to remember this moment.

After that, explore and clarify your values. What is the one thing that your soul desires across each area of your life? My soul craves peace, freedom, and joy. You may value love, happiness, and or security, to name a few.

Share your progress with myultimateself@estherlewars.com or use the hashtag #myultimateself on social media.

Exercise	Chapter
1	5 – Internalizing the Impact of Death
2	6 – Getting Beyond My Fears
3	7 – Death of A Parent
4	8 – Losing My Grandnephew
5	9 – A Community Service Partner
6	10 – Death of A Former Coworker
7	11 – Death As My Motivator
8	12 – Quantum Entanglement
9	13 – Taking Result-Oriented Actions
10	14 – I Have Favor, and So Do You
11 & 12	15 – Habits I Used to Win
13	16 – Retirement and Last Will

Exercise 1 – Chapter 5

Make a list of your first conversations surrounding death.

_____

_____

_____

_____

_____

How did those experiences make you feel? Give that version of yourself the necessary resources (a hug, a smile, compassion, empathy, etc.).

_____

_____

_____

_____

_____

_____

Exercise 2 – Chapter 6

What are your natural mental tendencies concerning death?

_____

_____

_____

_____

_____

What limiting beliefs did those thoughts create?

_____

_____

_____

_____

_____

Mentally change each thought to a positive image. Describe the revised image of yourself.

_____

_____

_____

_____

_____

_____

Exercise 3 – Chapter 7

Have you lost a loved one, such as a parent or caregiver? Write their name and at least one sentence describing who they were.

_____

_____

_____

_____

_____

How did this experience with death impact your life? What have you learned about yourself throughout this ordeal?

_____

_____

_____

_____

_____

Exercise 4 – Chapter 8

What was your second close experience with death, and how has it impacted your life?

_____

_____

_____

_____

_____

_____

What is at least one goal you can pursue to honor your loved one?

_____

_____

_____

_____

_____

What is second goal you can pursue to honor your loved one?

_____

_____

_____

_____

_____

_____

Exercise 5 – Chapter 9

Is there a person who passed away but made a lasting impression on your life? What was the lesson or insight that you learned from the person?

_____

_____

_____

_____

_____

What cause can you advocate for or support? Do you need to form an organization, or can you support an existing one?

_____

_____

_____

_____

_____

Exercise 6 – Chapter 10

Have you lost a close friend, associate, or co-worker? What was your experience, and how has it impacted your life?

_____

_____

_____

_____

_____

I pledge to take the following actions to promote joy in my life:

_____

_____

_____

_____

_____

_____

Remembering Your Special Person

Of all the losses we encounter, one person captured the essence of our being. They make us smile, laugh, and even cry when we think about them. Yes, they may have had flaws, but who doesn't? Use the space below to describe or draw pictures of the great qualities of that person.

Exercise 7 – Chapter 11

Have you ever lost yourself, physically or emotionally? At any point in life, what three actions or events made you realize that you were living below your God-given purpose?

_____

_____

_____

_____

_____

Complete the death visualization exercise and list at least three things you need to change.

_____

_____

_____

_____

_____

How would you feel if you implemented these changes?

_____

_____

_____

_____

_____

_____

Exercise 8 – Chapter 12

List your greatest fears.

_____

_____

_____

_____

_____

List your greatest aspirations.

_____

_____

_____

_____

_____

Exercise 9 – Chapter 13

Use the A.R.A.D.A.R. method to plan at least two goals. Reflect on your aspirations from exercise 8. Remember that your habits and actions will lead to achieving results.

PHASE	YOUR STATEMENT
Acceptance	
Reflection	
Awareness	
Decision	
Action	
Result	

Exercise 10 – Chapter 14

I am grateful for:

_____

_____

_____

_____

_____

I am grateful that I am:

_____

_____

_____

_____

_____

Exercise 11– Chapter 15

I will become:

_____

_____

_____

_____

_____

_____

_____

_____

_____

_____

_____

_____

_____

Exercise 12 – Chapter 15

To become, you must act and **Make Each Day Count.** Divide your year into 21-day segments.

1	2	3	4	5	6	7	8	9	10	11

Set a goal and check off each day that you work towards achieving it. If you get off track, no worries, just start over or keep going.

12	13	14	15	16	17	18	19	20	21	
										___
										___
										___
										___
										___
										___
										___
										___
										___
										___
										___
										___
										___
										___
										___
										___
										___
										___

Exercise 13 – Chapter 16

Use the below template to begin drafting your Last Will and Testament.

	YOUR INTENTIONS
INTRODUCTION (State full name and intent)	
EXECUTOR (Who will manage process?)	
BENEFICIARIES (Who will receive assets?)	
ASSETS (What will be distributed?)	
GUARDIANSHIP (Who will keep children?)	
FUNERAL ARRANGEMENTS (What are your desires?)	

Consult with a lawyer and plan to sign your finished will with two witnesses.

NOTES

1. All Bible verses are from the King James Version (KJV).

2. YouVersion Bible app provides daily verses; Bible Gateway offers easy search and access - www.biblegateway.com.

3. Most named towns are in New Jersey, USA

4. Photography by Esther Lewars - taken in Maplewood & Newark, except page 54, taken in Portland, Jamaica, at her dad's graveside.

5. Chapter 13 Reference - Intuition: Knowing Beyond Logic (Osho Insights for a New Way of Living) - Osho

6. In 2021, I enrolled in Tony Robins and Dean Graziozi's Project Next program. After completing this book, my Women Technology Confidence course will be available on the Mastermind platform.

7. Google Docs, Keep, and Voice Recording were valuable tools for journaling, writing, and collaborating with others on ideas.

8. Canva.com and Adobe CS were used for creative designs.

9. Grammarly and ChatGTP were used for review and editing.

10. YouTube has great self-education and personal growth videos.

11. Ancestry.com allowed me to connect with my ancestors.

12. Information Systems - open.lib.umn.edu/informationsystems.

13. Visit www.estherlewars.com for the worksheets and resources.

14. Send an email to info@estherlewars.com to share your feedback.

I will bless the Lord at all times: his praise shall continually be in my mouth.

Psalm 34:1 (KJV)

ABOUT THE AUTHOR

On March 18, 2023, Maxine Chin, Esther's eldest sister wrote the following paragraph to highlight the joy associated with Esther's birth and childhood. She wrote, "on March 18, 1978, a queen was born to Hermine and Reginald Birch in the beautiful Port Antonio, Portland, Jamaica. They called her Esther Elizabeth. Her three older siblings were happy to see this beautiful baby but were disappointed because they wanted a baby brother. Nevertheless, Queen Esther won their hearts, and they spoiled her rotten. I can still remember making her a pretty, red and white dress for her 3rd birthday and writing to Fae Ellington on the "Morning Ride" show on RJR for her to wish Esther a happy birthday. I let Esther listen to her name being called on the radio. Her cute little face lit up when she heard her name."

Esther was a pleasant and graceful child. Maxine was a significant influence on her upbringing. Her values and beliefs derived from modeling Maxine's desire for God, love, family, committed partnerships, hard work, and education. As a result, Maxine earned the title sister-mom. Esther is grateful for the years she lived with her in Ebony Vale, Spanish Town, St. Catherine, before migrating to the United States.

Esther emigrated to the United States as a teenager in 1995 and immediately focused on her education. She attended Newark Business

Training Institute and earned a Computer Applications Certificate. Her college journey started at Rutgers University-Newark & New Jersey Institute of Technology (NJIT), where she earned a Bachelor of Arts (B.A.) in Information Systems in 2000. In 2010, she graduated from Teachers College, Columbia University, with a Master of Arts (M.A.) in Computing in Education. She earned her Education Specialist degree (Ed.S.) in Education Leadership, Management, and Policy from Seton Hall University in 2017. She is a New Jersey licensed K-8 teacher, supervisor, principal, Kappi Delta Pi member, and a Google for Education Certified Trainer.

Esther Lewars is a compassionate, spiritually aware, lifelong learner and educator. Her extensive background as a technology coordinator, educational technology specialist, adjunct professor, and personal development expert has equipped her with the skills to lead in educational technology, information systems, and computer science education for over two decades.

She enjoyed creating systems to support a rich school technology infrastructure, provide teachers with professional development, and integrate technology in every classroom with every student in her school. As a district supervisor, she trains and supports staff in using students' data and information.

She is a proud mother to an 8th-grade son and an 11th-grade daughter. Both are mathematically and scientifically inclined. Alyssa is a great stage performer and tennis player. Ethan is a stolid man of power who plays lacrosse and enjoys working out.

Esther's personal and professional experiences with loss have inspired her to pursue self-development and were the driving force behind her first book. She enjoys dancing, listening to music, walking in nature, and being creative. In her class of 2000 yearbook, she aspired to establish a computer consulting firm in the US or Jamaica. As the founder of Vernov Technology Group, LLC, a digital media and training company, she is on her way to achieving that goal. Her contributions to local television programs such as NWK-TV Channel 28 and 78 have helped her to produce and share her knowledge and expertise with a broader audience.

For more information, visit www.estherlewars.com | @estherlewars

Made in the USA
Coppell, TX
11 April 2023

15495209R20095